PROMETHEUS

Carol Dougherty

Routledge
Taylor & Francis Group

LONDON AND NEW YORK

First published 2006
by Routledge
2 Park Square, Milton Park, Abingdon, Oxon OX14 4RN

Simultaneously published in the USA and Canada
by Routledge
270 Madison Ave, New York, NY 10016

Routledge is an imprint of the Taylor & Francis Group

Typeset in Utopia by Keystroke, Jacaranda Lodge, Wolverhampton
Printed and bound in Great Britain by TJ International Ltd, Padstow,
Cornwall

British Library Cataloguing in Publication Data
A catalogue record for this book is available from the British Library

Library of Congress Cataloging in Publication Data
Dougherty, Carol.
    Prometheus / Carol Dougherty.
        p. cm.
    Includes bibliographical references and index.
    ISBN 0–415–32405–X (hardback : alk. paper) —
    ISBN 0–415–32406–8 (pbk. : alk. paper)
    1. Prometheus (Greek deity) I. Title.
    BL820 .P68D68 2005
    292.2'113—dc22   2005009846

ISBN10: 0–415–32405–X (hbk)
ISBN10: 0–415–32406–8 (pbk)
ISBN13: 987–0–415–32405–2 (hbk)
ISBN13: 987–0–415–32406–9 (pbk)

For my family,
Joel, Nathan, and Megan

CONTENTS

SERIES FOREWORD

> For a person who is about to embark on any serious discourse or task, it is proper to begin first with the gods.
>
> (Demosthenes, *Letters* 1.1)

WHY GODS AND HEROES?

The gods and heroes of classical antiquity are part of our culture. Many function as sources of creative inspiration for poets, novelists, artists, composers, filmmakers and designers. Greek tragedy's enduring appeal has ensured an ongoing familiarity with its protagonists' experiences and sufferings, while the choice of Minerva as the logo of one of the newest British universities, the University of Lincoln, demonstrates the ancient gods' continued emblematic potential. Even the world of management has used them as representatives of different styles: Zeus and the 'club' culture for example, and Apollo and the 'role' culture: see C. Handy, *The Gods of Management: who they are, how they work and why they fail* (London, 1978).

This series is concerned with how and why these figures continue to fascinate and intrigue. But it has another aim too, namely to explore their strangeness. The familiarity of the gods and heroes risks obscuring a vital difference between modern meanings and ancient functions and purpose. With certain exceptions, people today do not worship them, yet to the Greeks and Romans they were real beings in a system comprising literally hundreds of divine powers. These range from the major gods, each of whom was worshipped in many guises via their epithets or 'surnames', to the heroes – deceased individuals associated with local communities – to other figures such as daimons and nymphs. The landscape was dotted with sanctuaries, while natural features such as mountains, trees and rivers were thought to be inhabited by religious beings. Studying ancient paganism involves finding strategies to comprehend a world where everything was, in the often quoted words of Thales, 'full of gods'.

In order to get to grips with this world, it is necessary to set aside our preconceptions of the divine, shaped as they are in large part by Christianised notions of a transcendent, omnipotent God who is morally good. The Greeks and Romans worshipped numerous beings, both male and female, who looked, behaved and suffered like humans, but who, as immortals, were not bound by the human condition. Far from being omnipotent, each had limited powers: even the sovereign, Zeus/Jupiter, shared control of the universe with his brothers Poseidon/Neptune (the sea) and Hades/Pluto (the under-world). Lacking a creed or anything like an organised church, ancient paganism was open to continual reinterpretation, with the result that we should not expect to find figures with a uniform essence. It is common to begin accounts of the pantheon with a list of the major gods and their function(s) (Hephaistos/Vulcan: craft; Aphrodite/Venus: love; and Artemis/Diana: the hunt and so on), but few are this straightforward. Aphrodite, for example is much more than the goddess of love, vital though that function is. Her epithets include *Hetaira* ('courtesan') and *Porne* ('prostitute'), but also attest roles as varied as patron of the citizen body (*Pandemos*: 'of all the people') and protectress of seafaring (*Euploia, Pontia, Limenia*).

Recognising this diversity, the series consists not of biographies of each god or hero (though such have been attempted in the past), but of investigations into their multifaceted aspects within the complex world of ancient paganism. Its approach has been shaped partly in response to two distinctive patterns in previous research. Until the middle of the twentieth century, scholarship largely took the form of studies of individual gods and heroes. Many works presented a detailed appraisal of such issues as each figure's origins, myth and cult; these include L.R. Farnell's examination of major deities in his *Cults of the Greek States* (5 vols, Oxford, 1896–1909) and A.B. Cook's huge three-volume *Zeus* (Cambridge, 1914–40). Others applied theoretical developments to the study of gods and heroes, notably (and in the closest existing works to a uniform series) K. Kerényi in his investigations of gods as Jungian archetypes, including *Prometheus: archetypal image of human existence* (English trans. London 1963) and *Dionysos: archetypal image of the indestructable life* (English trans. London 1976).

In contrast, under the influence of French structuralism, the later part of the century saw a deliberate shift away from research into particular gods and heroes towards an investigation of the system of which they were part. Fuelled by a conviction that the study of isolated gods could not do justice to the dynamics of ancient religion, the pantheon came to be represented as a logical and coherent network in which the various powers were systematically opposed to one another. In a classic study by J.-P. Vernant, for example, the Greek concept of space was shown to be consecrated through the opposition between Hestia (goddess of the hearth – fixed space) and Hermes (messenger and traveller god – moveable space): Vernant, *Myth and Thought Among the Greeks*, London, 1983, 127–75). The gods as individual entities were far from neglected however, as may be exemplified by the works by Vernant, and his colleague M. Detienne, on particular deities including Artemis, Dionysos and Apollo: see, most recently, Detienne's *Apollon, le couteau en main: une approche expérimentale du polythéisme grec* (Paris, 1998).

In a sense, this series is seeking a middle ground. While approaching its subjects as unique (if diverse) individuals, it pays attention to their significance as powers within the collectivity of religious beings. *Gods and Heroes of the Ancient World* sheds new light on many of the most important religious beings of classical antiquity; it also provides a route into understanding Greek and Roman polytheism in the twenty-first century.

The series is intended to interest the general reader as well as being geared to the needs of students in a wide range of fields from Greek and Roman religion and mythology, classical literature and anthropology, to Renaissance literature and cultural studies. Each book presents an authoritative, accessible and refreshing account of its subject via three main sections. The introduction brings out what it is about the god or hero that merits particular attention. This is followed by a central section which introduces key themes and ideas, including (to varying degrees) origins, myth, cult and representations in literature and art. Recognising that the heritage of myth is a crucial factor in its continued appeal, the reception of each figure since antiquity forms the subject of the third part of the book. The volumes include illustrations of each god/hero and where appropriate time charts, family trees and maps. An annotated bibliography synthesises past research and indicates useful follow-up reading.

For convenience, the masculine terms 'gods' and 'heroes' have been selected for the series title, although (and with an apology for the male-dominated language), the choice partly reflects ancient usage in that the Greek *theos* ('god') is used of goddesses too. For convenience and consistency, Greek spellings are used for ancient names, except for famous Latinised exceptions, and BC/AD has been selected rather than BCE/CE.

I am indebted to Catherine Bousfield, the editorial assistant until 2004, who (literally) dreamt up the series and whose thoroughness and motivation brought it close to its launch. The hard work and efficiency of her successor, Matthew Gibbons, has overseen its progress to publication, and the classics editor of Routledge, Richard Stoneman, has provided support and expertise throughout. The anonymous readers for each proposal gave frank and helpful advice, while the authors' commitment to advancing scholarship while producing accessible accounts of their designated subjects has made it a pleasure to work with them.

Susan Deacy, Roehampton University, June 2005

ACKNOWLEDGEMENTS

First and foremost, I owe an intellectual debt of gratitude to Richard P. Martin, from whom I have learned most of what I know about Greek myth. He brings a rare combination of scholarly erudition and good common sense to his study of myth, and I have tried to put what I have learned from him to good use in this book.

As always, I want to thank my good friend and collaborator, Leslie Kurke, for her encouragement and editing help, especially with the Greek chapters. Closer to home, I want to thank my Wellesley colleague, Brendon Reay, for reading several chapters and, more generally, for listening to me think out loud this past year. My other colleagues in Classical Studies at Wellesley have listened to a great deal about Prometheus as well and given me invaluable bibliographical guidance – Mary Lefkowitz, Ray Starr, Miranda Marvin, and Elizabeth Greene. Jens Kruse, in the German department, was helpful in the early stages of my work on Goethe. I owe huge thanks to two students in the department, Cori Gentilesco and especially Joanna Theiss, for their tireless work and incredible initiative in finding, requesting, and keeping track of the illustrations that appear here. Mary Lefkowitz deserves an additional acknowledgement and heartfelt thanks for her eleventh-hour assistance in tracking down etymologies and scanning images. My work on this project was supported in part by a faculty research grant from Wellesley College.

I also want to thank my colleagues across the Atlantic, Paul Cartledge and Lorna Hardwick, for their help in supplying me with texts, reviews, and even the video itself of Tony Harrison's *Prometheus*, allowing me to make Harrison's work an integral part of this book.

This project has given me the opportunity to pull together my thoughts on Greek myth in an exciting new context, and I want to thank Susan Deacy, the series editor, for inviting me to take part in this new series. Thanks, too, go to Catherine Bousfield and Matthew Gibbons, the Routledge editors for this project – their patience and logistical help were much appreciated.

And last, but not least, I want to thank my husband, Joel Krieger, whose enthusiasm for Prometheus and coal mining got me started on this project and whose expertise in editing helped me finish it. It wouldn't be the same book without his help, good humour, and intelligence.

DISCLAIMER

EXCERPTS

ILLUSTRATIONS

GENEALOGICAL TABLE

THE GENERATION OF TITANS

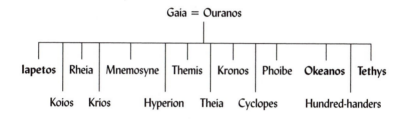

Gaia = Ouranos

Iapetos | Rheia | Mnemosyne | Themis | Kronos | Phoibe | Okeanos | Tethys

Koios   Krios   Hyperion   Theia   Cyclopes   Hundred-handers

THE FAMILY OF PROMETHEUS

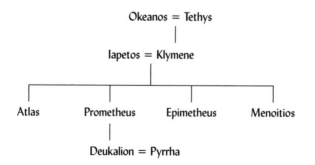

Okeanos = Tethys

Iapetos = Klymene

Atlas   Prometheus   Epimetheus   Menoitios

Deukalion = Pyrrha

WHY PROMETHEUS?

INTRODUCING PROMETHEUS

Myths and legends about Prometheus, the Greek god who defied Zeus to steal fire for humankind, thrive in art and literature from archaic Greece to modern times. As rebel, traitor, culture hero, and protector of mankind, Prometheus embodies the human condition with all its potential for brilliant innovation and for cruel suffering. Throughout the centuries since the Prometheus myth first captured the popular imagination, the fire that he steals for mortals has come to represent the spirit of technology, forbidden knowledge, the conscious intellect, political power, and artistic inspiration. As a god whose name means 'forethought,' Prometheus signals mortals' repeated attempts to overcome the limitations of their knowledge about the future – hope, technology, and prophecy are all part of Prometheus' complicated gift to mankind.

In other words, although some traditions do present Prometheus as the actual creator of mankind, the essence of the Prometheus myth is much broader and more heuristic – it has helped people from the time of Hesiod to the present to explore, question, and challenge the limits of the human condition. While Greek myth in general is known for the ease with which it can be transported to new and different texts and contexts, the myth of Prometheus is an extraordinarily flexible one. Time and time again, at moments of both dire oppression and limitless optimism, Prometheus is called upon to help us think about what it means to be human. In this book we will take a close look at several poets and writers, both ancient and modern, who place Prometheus at the centre of their own works. What are the essential, non-negotiable elements of Prometheus' myth? How does it evolve in response to different historical and cultural contexts? Most important, why does the god who stole fire for mankind continue to fascinate us more than two thousand five hundred years after he first burst on the scene in archaic Greece?

WHO IS PROMETHEUS?

But first, some background – who is Prometheus? What did he do? One source of information about Prometheus is his very name since it, like his myth, has generated a rich set of etymological explanations from authors from the archaic Greek poet Hesiod to the present. Prometheus' name is a compound proper noun, the first half of which is easily derived from *pro* – meaning 'before'. The second part, however, like the god himself, is tricky. One possibility is to derive it from *metis*, cognate with the verb *medomai*, meaning 'clever intelligence' to explain Prometheus' name as 'the one who thinks in advance'. This is surely the etymology that Hesiod had in mind when he invented Epimetheus (late-thinker) as the name for Prometheus' dim-witted brother in his cosmological poem, *Theogony*. The fifth-century Athenian playwright, Aeschylus, introduces similar etymological word play with Prometheus' name into his drama, *Prometheus Bound*. While the Greeks clearly understood Prometheus' name as 'forethinker', recent work in linguistics links the *meth* component to a Sanskrit root *math* – meaning to steal – suggesting that the actual etymology refers to theft, no doubt of fire, and links the Greek Prometheus myth with other similar myths from the Caucasus.

Literary (and other) texts, of course, provide us with a much fuller sense of Prometheus' story. In the *Theogony*, Hesiod tells us that Prometheus is one of three sons born to the Titan Iapetos and Klymene, one of the daughters of Ocean:

> Then Iapetos led away a daughter of Ocean,
> Klymene, pretty ankles, and went to bed with her.
> And she bore him a child, Atlas, stout heart,
> And begat ultraglorious Menoitios, and Prometheus,

Complex, his mind a shimmer, and witless Epimetheus,
Who was trouble from the start for enterprising men,
First to accept from Zeus the fabricated woman,
The Maiden.

(*Theogony* 507–14, trans. Lombardo 1993)

This maiden, of course, is Pandora whose jar full of evils has brought trouble and sickness to mankind ever since. Some traditions name Asia, instead of Klymene, as Prometheus' mother; others claim Asia was his wife. Another fragment of Hesiod's poetry mentions that Prometheus had a son, Deukalion, and the Roman poet Ovid tells us that when Zeus flooded the earth in anger, Deukalion and his wife Pyrrha, following in the footsteps of his father, (re-)created humans by throwing stones over their shoulders from which people sprung up. 'And from this,' Ovid concludes the tale, 'we are a hard race, experienced in work, and we give proof of the origins from which we are born.' (*Metamorphoses* 1.414–15)

As for the story of Prometheus, himself, we find the following succinct summary within the mythographer Apollodorus' (c. 186–120 BC) collection of Greek mythic traditions:

Prometheus moulded men from water and earth and gave them also fire, hiding it from Zeus in a fennel stalk. But when Zeus learned of it, he ordered Hephaestus to nail his body to Mount Caucasus (this is a Scythian mountain). On it Prometheus was nailed and bound for many years. Each day an eagle swooped on him and ate the lobes of his liver, which grew back each night. And Prometheus paid this penalty for the theft of fire until Hercules released him later, as we will make clear in the section on Hercules.

(Apollodorus, *Library* I.vii.1)

Apollodorus' account is reassuringly comprehensive – it gives us a coherent story that unites and explains all the different elements of Prometheus' myth. This sense of completeness can be misleading, however, since no Greek of the archaic or classical period would ever have encountered such a rational and comprehensive version of Prometheus' mythic career. Instead, the ancient Greek reader may have found something like the following explanation of Zeus' harsh punishment of Prometheus from Hesiod's *Theogony*:

> That happened when the gods and mortal men were negotiating
> At Mekone. Prometheus cheerfully butchered a great ox
> And served it up, trying to befuddle Zeus' wits.
> For Zeus he set out flesh and innards rich with fat
> Laid out on the oxhide and covered with its paunch.
> But for the others he set out the animal's white bones
> Artfully dressed out and covered with shining fat.
>
> (*Theogony* 535–41, trans. Lombardo 1993)

Here, as we will see in chapter 1, Hesiod emphasizes Prometheus' role as the inventor of sacrifice, a key institution that dominates Greek religious and public life, as the defining moment in Prometheus' story. And yet, sacrifice is rarely mentioned in any of the other extant treatments from antiquity. Consider, for example, the following dialogue between Prometheus and the chorus of Oceanids in Aeschylus' *Prometheus Bound*. Prometheus is shackled to a mountain crag at the beginning of the play, and when the chorus ask what he did to deserve such punishment, he gives a very different answer:

> P: I stopped mortals from foreseeing their fate.
> Ch: What kind of cure did you discover for this sickness?
> P: Blind hopes I placed in them.
> Ch: This is a great benefit you gave to men.
> P: Besides this, I gave them fire.
> Ch: And now do creatures of the day possess bright-faced fire?
> P: Yes, from which they will learn many skills.
>
> (*Prometheus Bound* 248–54)

In this version – and we will explore this further in chapter 3 – the gifts of hope and fire, not sacrifice, are at the heart of Prometheus' myth. A story attributed to the legendary fabulist, Aesop, however, mentions neither the invention of sacrifice nor the theft of fire, focusing instead on Prometheus' creation of mankind as a way to explain certain personality traits in humans:

> Following Zeus' orders, Prometheus fashioned humans and animals. When Zeus
> saw that the animals far outnumbered the humans, he ordered Prometheus to

Figure 1 Goltzius, *Prometheus Making Man*

Source: Photo courtesy of Davison Art Center, Wesleyan University

reduce the number of the animals by turning them into people. Prometheus did as he was told, and as a result those people who were originally animals have a human body but the soul of an animal.

(Fable 515, trans. Gibbs 2002)

As we can see from this brief overview of ancient sources, far from having any kind of fixed or canonical status, the myth of Prometheus is infinitely flexible. Neither Hesiod, Aeschylus, nor Aesop recounts the entire story of Prometheus from beginning to end, as Apollodorus does. Instead, each author selects and highlights a particular theme or element of the myth to elaborate within a specific literary or cultural context. And yet, in each case, everyone knows which Prometheus we are talking about. Many post-classical writers and artists have made use of Prometheus' myth selectively as well. The elasticity and flexibility of Prometheus' myth are among its most striking features – and this process is never-ending.

The German Romantic poet Goethe offers a variation of Prometheus as creator of mankind in the concluding lines of his poem 'Prometheus,' spoken by the god himself:

Here I sit, forming men
In my image,
A race to resemble me:
To suffer, to weep,
To enjoy, to be glad –
And never to heed you,
Like me!

For Goethe, as we will see in chapter 4, Prometheus functions as both a symbol of human defiance and of poetic creativity, and so the creation of mankind is the part of Prometheus' myth that he chooses to elaborate. The English poet laureate, Ted Hughes (1930–98) returned again and again to the richness of Prometheus' myth in a collection of poems that take the Titan's story as the jumping off point for further meditation on the human experience. Here's just one example from *Prometheus on his Crag*:

Prometheus on his crag
Began to admire the vulture
It knew what it was doing

It went on doing it
Swallowing not only his liver
But managing also to digest its guilt

And hang itself again just under the sun
Like a heavenly weighing scales
Balancing the gift of life

And the cost of the gift
Without a tremor
As if both were nothing.

(Hughes 2003)

Hughes omits the bulk of Prometheus's story – no sacrifice, theft, or creation – and instead zooms in on the god in his state of perpetual punishment, imagining the moment of confronting the consequences of one's actions extended for thirty thousand years. The twentieth-century Australian poet, A.D. Hope, radically rewrites the conclusion of Prometheus' myth, giving us an idea of just how elastic his myth can be. Towards the end of a poem entitled 'Prometheus Unbound' a still fettered Prometheus catches sight of Hermes swooping down from the heavens to strike his chains. But when the Titan asks whether Zeus has either relented or been forced from power, Hermes replies:

'His wisdom is not mocked,' the god replied,
'Nor alters nor repeals the great decree.
These are his words: "Go, set the Titan free;
And let his torment be to wander wide
The ashes of mankind from sea to sea,
Judging that theft of fire from which they died."'
(Hope 1966, *Prometheus Bound*: 9–14)

Hope thus reverses some of the key elements of Prometheus' myth, and yet, the myth remains unchanged. Prometheus' liberation (by

Hermes here, not Heracles) has become, in the end, a new formulation of his eternal punishment – as well as that of mankind.

For poets like Goethe, Hughes, or Hope, as for the ancients, the myth of Prometheus (and others) is infinitely flexible, a gold mine of poetic possibilities. Precisely because it does not need to be recounted in detail, the myth offers the poet a wealth of themes and questions about the human experience to be elaborated, extended, questioned, even overturned. Outside of mythological handbooks like that of Apollodorus (or the more modern versions), Greek myths are never told from beginning to end, and the elements of a myth that are omitted are just as significant as those that are included. Precisely because everyone already knows the stories, they are always only partially retold.

CLASSIC TEXTS: THE WELLSPRING OF MYTHS

The myth of Prometheus holds these features of selective and partial retelling in common with other classical myths. Homer's epic poem the *Iliad* recounts the events of a mere ten days of the tenth year of the Trojan War. The *Odyssey* picks up the story of just one hero returning home after the war is over. Neither poem recounts the Trojan War from beginning to end. Nowhere in either poem will you find an account of the rape of Helen, the sacrifice of Iphigenia, the expedition to Troy, or the death of Achilles. Instead, each poem assumes a rich and complex narrative tradition and improvises within it. The poet of the *Odyssey* asks the Muse to 'start somewhere' in the story of Odysseus' return, and the audience, we can assume, derives its pleasure from a particularly good (and perhaps surprisingly new) variation upon a well-known theme. The Hollywood movie *Troy* (2004) offers a contemporary example of this phenomenon. While its seemingly reckless indifference to the canonical influence of Homer has infuriated many a viewer, professional classicists and amateurs alike, its unusual take on the story may be more 'authentic' than we realize at first. As did Homer, the makers of *Troy* adapted the age-old myth to suit the taste and interests of a contemporary audience.

This principle of selectivity is especially applicable to the study of the Prometheus myth. In fact, of all the myths from classical antiquity, Prometheus' may be the most flexible. Nowhere (outside Apollodorus) is it told straight through from beginning to end, and so it is critical that we note the difference between a myth and the text in which it is embedded. The myth of Prometheus forms the basis for Aeschylus' *Prometheus Bound*, but the myth is not synonymous with the play. Aeschylus' drama offers us just one reading of it – a particularly powerful one to be sure, but a very different reading from the one we find in, say, the British Romantic poet Percy Bysshe Shelley's play, *Prometheus Unbound*, or on a mural painted by the twentieth-century Mexican muralist José Clemente Orozco.

It is also important to recognize that the text in which a myth like that of Prometheus appears need not be a conventional written document. On the contrary, Prometheus, like many mythic figures, appears on Greek vase paintings, Roman sarcophagi, in the paintings of Renaissance masters – even as part of the advertising portfolios of twentieth-century companies. He has lent his name to a contemporary dance troop, a moon of Jupiter, medical technology companies, and a kind of cigarette lighter. We might say that the 'authoritative' version of a given Greek myth is both everywhere and nowhere. Since the story material is already there, embedded within the cultural memory, each teller is free to innovate, to retell the myth anew.

WHAT IS MYTH?

One way that we use the term 'myth' today is to refer to something that was once believed but now has been 'disproved'. Myths are the stories of the past, the quaint attempts of ancient or primitive cultures to explain the mysterious ways of their worlds. Modern cultures often claim to have replaced these creative and fantastic accounts of humans born from stones or sun-gods driving chariots with objective historical narratives and scientific explanations. Moreover, the concept of myth is often conflated with specific mythic traditions, especially those of ancient Greece and Rome, and thereby excluded from contemporary consideration as legitimate or informative narrative accounts.

Following from this belief that we have outgrown myths in the modern world, the term 'myth' is sometimes used pejoratively to dismiss accounts as demonstrably false or misleading. Horatio Alger's mid-nineteenth-century accounts of heroic struggles for success helped inspire the American dream that hard work – rather than accidents of birth – determined where one ended up in society. When people today refer, then, to the 'myth of Horatio Alger', they imply that upward mobility is not as easy to achieve as Alger made it seem. Similarly, those who see the European Union reaching into nearly every area of public policy in each of its member states, limiting their authority to control their own destiny, may reasonably refer to the 'myth of sovereignty' or perhaps even the 'myth of the nation-state'.

But myth is not synonymous with unproven assertions or misleading historical claims; nor does it belong exclusively to traditional cultures from long ago. People from all cultures tell myths – even highly rational citizens of the twenty-first century do so. Myths – such as the heroic unity of Britons withstanding the Blitz – help us think about what it means to be who we are. And yet, myth is a notoriously difficult concept to define. It can be traced etymologically to the Greek word *muthos*, which in Homer designates a kind of authoritative speech, one that demands action and commands respect. Agamemnon's speech to the troops in Book 2 of the *Iliad* is such a *muthos*; Nestor's speech recalling his youth is another. Embedded within an oral tradition, these stories rely on depictions of the past and celebrations of the famous deeds of glorious ancestors as a source for their moral and cultural authority. Once alphabetic writing was introduced to the Greek world in the mid eighth century BC and different versions of these stories could be written down and compared, the meaning of *muthos* began to shift away from authoritative utterances to include something like fiction or lie as well. The next step, of course, is for Greek thinkers to begin to criticize these myths and to look to other modes of discourse to explain the world and their place in it. This is not to say, however, that we can trace a clear trajectory from myth (*muthos*) to rational argument (*logos*), or even begin to make a systematic distinction between them. The tales that the fourth-century BC philosopher Plato banishes from his ideal *Republic*, after all, are called *logoi*, and he often turns to *muthoi* within what we might call the more rational arguments of his philosophical dialogues to make an important point.

At the very least, then, myth is a problematic category – both for us and for the Greeks. Some scholars have even argued that the term *muthos* did not designate a specific type of narrative or mode of thought in ancient Greece, that it did not function as an indigenous narrative category. In any event, myth is not something that belongs exclusively to the ancient Greeks – all cultures, ancient and modern, Western and non-Western, tell myths. Instead of looking to Greek etymology or literature for an authoritative definition, then, we must define myth more broadly as the kind of story that people in a culture find compelling.

WHY ARE MYTHS SO IMPORTANT?

Myths take on the role of shaping a society's imagination. To borrow a concept from the cultural anthropologist Clifford Geertz, myths provide a common body of material that is not only important to think about but also 'good to think with' (Geertz 1973: 23). The myth of the Trojan War, for example, offered the fifth-century Athenians a rich context for interrogating the horrors of war and refining their notions of heroism at a time when they were embroiled in nearly a half-century of hostilities with Sparta. In this respect, I suggest that we think of myth not as an object or an idea, but rather as a system of communication that depends on a body of pre-worked material, a system that brings with it a host of associations, connotations, and interpretive baggage. A key component of this culturally rich material within Greek myth are the gods and goddesses. The role of the Olympian gods and goddesses in myth and literature is notoriously hard for contemporary readers much more familiar with monotheistic religious traditions to understand. On the one hand, the deities of Greek mythology are the same figures that form the backbone of Greek religion – Zeus, Aphrodite, Ares, and Prometheus, for example, all have cults and festivals in their honour as part of a pantheistic religious system. On the other hand, however, these same gods can and do appear in literary, artistic, and historical narratives that transcend this religious context, narrowly defined. Artemis and Aphrodite, for example, appear in Euripides' tragedy *Hippolytus* to help the audience think about the continuum of sexual experience, from total abstinence to incestuous rape. Similarly, when Zeus appears in Aeschylus' play *Prometheus Bound*, he needs no introduction. He brings with him his status as king of gods and men, his personal relationships (marriage with Metis), his past exploits (defeat of Titans), and his areas of power and influence (intelligence, strength, political authority).

Myth, then, is powerful precisely because it can take all this pre-worked, culturally rich material – gods, goddesses, plots, and places – and work with it to create a narrative that is important and compelling to its audience. Myth is not always synonymous with religion, and, in fact, when religious figures are employed in myths, they are often employed for distinctly secular reasons. Literary (or artistic) texts that draw upon Greek myth will inevitably populate their texts with divine figures that operate more heuristically than religiously – they are 'good to think with' about important issues like war, sexuality, or progress.

As a vibrant system of communication rather than as a static collection of stories, myths play an important role within a culture over time. Above all, they help cultures accommodate and negotiate change in a productive way. In this respect we might think about the relationship between myth and history along the following lines suggested by the French literary theorist Roland Barthes:

> What the world supplies to myth is an historical reality, defined, even if this goes back quite a while, by the way in which men have produced or used it; and what myth gives in return is a *natural* image of this reality.

> (Barthes [1957] 1972: 142)

Over the course of this book, we will see the ways that the myth of Prometheus continues to be told in a variety of very different historical contexts – archaic and classical Greece, the years following the French Revolution, and late twentieth-century England. We will see that each time the Prometheus myth is told, as Barthes suggests, the specific historical circumstances give it a very different kind of reality. And yet, in the end, the real force of the myth is to make that specific historical context seem natural each time – the only way things could possibly be.

THE MYTH OF PROMETHEUS

Because of the innate flexibility of myth, we will need to look to a range of texts to sketch out the parameters of the plot of the Prometheus myth for the ancient Greeks. There is no mention of Prometheus in the Homeric poems so we must look to the works of the archaic poet Hesiod for our first sighting of the Greek god who stole fire for mankind. Hesiod includes Prometheus' story in two of the poetic works attributed to him: the *Theogony* and the *Works and Days*. In the *Theogony*, Hesiod explains that Prometheus helped mankind establish the institution of sacrifice by tricking Zeus into accepting the lesser portion of fat and bones. When Zeus hid fire from man in punishment, Prometheus stole it back from the Olympian gods and gave it to humans, for which act both he and they were severely punished. In the *Works and Days*, Hesiod tells in more detail how Zeus sent down the first woman, Pandora, to humans as payment for fire, and in the *Theogony*, he recounts how Prometheus was bound to the Caucasus mountains where an eagle devoured his ever-regenerating liver daily until Heracles appeared to liberate him from this torture.

Early iconographical sources for the Prometheus myth also emphasize these two stages of the story: Prometheus' punishment for the theft of fire and his eventual release at the hands of Heracles. The earliest visual representations of the myth are roughly contemporary with Hesiod's poems (mid-seventh century BC) and focus on Prometheus' punishment. Prometheus appears on a Greek gem, for example, with his hands tied behind his back, crouching down in front of a long-winged bird. In the sixth century BC, we find representations of Prometheus' liberation by Heracles on Attic and Etruscan vases. On an amphora currently in Berlin, Prometheus again crouches facing the eagle, but this time Heracles is shown behind Prometheus shooting an arrow at the bird. A Laconian cup (c. 550 BC), currently in the Vatican Museum, shows Prometheus together with his brother Atlas as twin victims of Zeus' anger (Fig. 2). Atlas stands hunched over

Figure 2 Atlas and Prometheus, inv. 16592. Laconian cup, c. 550 BC
Source: Photo courtesy of Photographic Archives, Vatican, Rome

bearing the burden of the sky upon his shoulders while Prometheus is shown seated with the eagle on his lap feasting on his liver.

After Hesiod, it is not until the fifth century that we find another extended literary treatment of the Prometheus myth. The Athenian tragedian Aeschylus draws upon the story of Prometheus' theft of fire from Zeus and subsequent gift to mankind in his play, *Prometheus Bound*. The play, which may have formed part of a trilogy devoted to the Prometheus myth, locates the myth within a larger conflict between the Titan and Zeus and uses it to celebrate humanity's progress away from the primitive state of animals towards a greater civilized life. We also have evidence that Aeschylus wrote a satyr play called *Prometheus Fire-Kindler*, which together with some fifth-century vase paintings appears to focus less on his punishment and more specifically on his gift of fire to mankind.

The story that Prometheus creates mankind from mud or clay must have been known in Athens, perhaps as early as the fifth century BC. A fable attributed to Aesop that may date as early as the classical period says that 'The clay which Prometheus used when he fashioned man was not mixed with water but with tears' (Fable 516, trans. Gibbs 2002). This reference suggests that a version of Prometheus as creator was already in circulation at this time. And yet while the creation aspect of Prometheus may have been known, it is interesting that it did not form the basis of a major literary or artistic work in the archaic or classical Greek world. The story is only briefly mentioned by the comic poets Menander and Philemon in the fourth century BC. Prometheus, creator of mankind, does appear on Etruscan or Italic gems from the third and second centuries BC, however, and the theme is taken up with enthusiasm by the Roman poets of the Augustan period. Ovid opens his *Metamorphoses* with an account of the creation of the earth, including Prometheus fashioning man from water and earth:

> which, mixed with rain water, the son of Iapetos fashioned into the form of the gods who control everything. And while the other animals are prone and look down to the earth, he gave to man an uplifted face and ordered him to look to the heaven and to turn his face to the stars. In this way, the earth which had been rough and formless was changed and took on the previously unknown forms of men.
>
> (*Metamorphoses* 1.82–88)

The Roman lyric poets, Catullus, Horace, and Propertius, too, allude to Prometheus as the creator of humans.

In addition to poetic depictions, visual images of Prometheus creating mankind attracted the Romans and appear especially in funeral contexts. The Capitoline Sarcophagus, for example, from the Villa Doria Pamphili combines the Platonic notion of Prometheus stealing fire from Vulcan's workshop with Aeschylus' liberation of Prometheus and an elaborate depiction of the journey of the soul. In this respect, the Promethean myth of creation offers a visual symbol of the Neoplatonic dualistic concept of the body and the soul as well as influencing Christian traditions of the origins of mankind.

A composite of the myth of Prometheus thus emerges fairly clearly from antiquity: Prometheus stole fire from the gods and gave it to humans; he was punished for his actions and subsequently liberated by Heracles. He is also said to have created humans from clay and water, animating these creatures with fire. Why do artists, writers, poets, and playwrights continue to return to Prometheus' story time and again? What are the key issues and most compelling themes that have emerged from 2,500 years of reflection on Prometheus and the human condition?

PROMETHEAN THEMES: FIRE, REBELLION, CREATIVITY, AND WORK

Fire, of course, is at the heart of Prometheus' story, and Prometheus is often portrayed, in ancient and modern times, proudly holding a torch overhead. Fire and the technology that it makes possible are at once the source of civilized life, giving mankind freedom from the constraints of nature – warmth in cold winters, light in darkness, cooked not raw food – and the historic tools of devastation and destruction. Many of the poets and artists whose work we will be considering focus on this fundamental ambiguity at the heart of Prometheus' gift of fire. Fire provides mankind with the means, both material and spiritual, to develop all those technologies and skills that mark his existence as superior to that of the beasts. And yet, from classical Athens to twentieth-century Europe, mankind has looked to the very same Prometheus to acknowledge fire's devastating potential to return us and the earth we inhabit to a pre-civilized era.

Prometheus' gift of fire is a stolen gift, and in his series of essays *Thieves of Fire* the literary critic Denis Donoghue offers some interesting speculations about the implications of this aspect of the myth – an element that appears to be universal. He notes that with a true gift, a relationship is established between two parties, the donor and the recipient, but with a stolen gift, a third party, the original owner, emerges. This raises important questions about the relationship between the original owner and the recipient – in this case, between Zeus and mankind. To what extent is mankind implicated in Prometheus' crime against Zeus? If a gift has been stolen, can its recipient ever release itself from its origins in violence?

The myth of Prometheus thus always begins with an act of transgression, and it sketches out a complicated three-way relationship. Prometheus does not just give man fire, but he steals it for him and by stealing the fire from Zeus, Prometheus rebels against the powers that be. This revolutionary aspect of Prometheus' myth has been a powerful one from the very beginning and it takes on multiple forms: Prometheus steals fire, creates humans, helps cheat Zeus with sacrifice, and keeps secrets from him. At heart, Prometheus is a rebel, and he helps represent those without power in an ongoing battle against tyranny and authoritarian regimes of all kinds. At the same time, however, Prometheus functions as a kind of scapegoat – the one responsible for the difficulties and miseries of mankind. As we noted above, his actions have consequences – not just for him, but also for mankind – and Prometheus is thus also implicated in the suffering that marks the human experience.

This element of suffering is often important to Prometheus' creative efforts as well – we remember that Aesop made this connection by noting that Prometheus moulded mankind from mud and tears. Some look to art to alleviate or address the inevitable misery at the heart of the human experience, articulating the suffering of mankind or a powerful sense of defiance, or both. Others cast their own creative efforts in a Promethean light – looking to the god as a model for their own artistic endeavours. Still others take Prometheus' gift of fire to be symbolic of the imaginative powers of the artist. And yet, as with all aspects of Prometheus' legacy to mankind, the creative impulse can be a dangerous one as well, and Prometheus has been invoked to question the limits of the human ability to meddle with the divine spark of creation – in artistic, technological, and medical terms.

Finally, Prometheus' story is that of the working man. Before Prometheus, humans did not have to work – in the Golden Age, the earth gave its fruit freely to mankind and the living was easy. But once Prometheus stole fire, Zeus punished mankind for his gift by withholding this comfortable means of existence. Ever since, Prometheus has come to symbolize man's need to work – whether it is the back-breaking subsistence agriculture of archaic Greece, the skill applied by Athenian craftsmen in the potter's quarter, or the daily grind of dull and debilitating work in a factory during the industrial revolution. Both his revolutionary history as well as his association with human labour make Prometheus the perfect figure for thinking about the role of work in the human experience over the ages – exploitation of workers by management, abusive working conditions, and more.

PROMETHEUS AND THE HUMAN CONDITION

As the thief of fire, rebel against authority, creator of mankind, and patron saint of work, Prometheus helps us come to terms with the nature, scope, and evolution of the human condition in all its fundamental complexity. One of the most richly ambiguous in all of Greek mythology, Prometheus' myth has been invoked to tell a story of the human condition as a celebration of the triumph of the human intellect, imagination, and technology over all that nature can throw our way. And yet, Prometheus' myth has also been called upon to explain why it is that backbreaking toil, oppressive political conditions, and endless suffering define our daily life.

How can one and the same myth generate such wildly divergent narratives of the human condition? Rather than glorifying or lamenting any one single version of the human experience, again and again, Prometheus and his mythic plot provide the interpretive framework for thinking about what it means to be human at specific times for specific groups of people. Each time the story that Prometheus' myth generates is particular to the culture and experience of the people who tell it. It is not that the myth of Prometheus changes, but rather the nature of the human experience that he comes to represent has changed. No more than Aphrodite glorifies the notion of love or Ares the institution of war, Prometheus does not glorify the human condition. Rather, like all truly influential mythic figures, Prometheus helps us reflect upon and even reimagine our own human experience. His myth, to return to Barthes' formulation, helps naturalize – and thus to make sense of – whatever set of circumstances history has dealt a given people. Prometheus, the god whose gift to humanity includes hope, gives us ways to cope with the uncertainty that accompanies the human experience. As mere mortals with but partial knowledge of our world, we can only guess at what it means to be human, and the etymology of Prometheus' name as 'forethought' has always been an important part of his myth.

SURVEY OF SCHOLARSHIP AND OVERVIEW OF THE BOOK

For these reasons the myth of Prometheus, first articulated in archaic Greece, continues to come to the fore at significant moments in history. Above all, this book will ask how Prometheus helps different cultures at different times think about what it means to be human. Carl Kerényi's (1963) book on Prometheus, although dated somewhat by its Jungian approach to Prometheus as an 'archetypal image of human existence', remains an important contribution to the study of Prometheus as a mythic figure from the ancient world to that of Goethe. Aside from Kerényi's book, scholarship on Prometheus has primarily taken two directions. The masterful treatments of Louis Séchan and Raymond Trousson, for example, provide comprehensive surveys of the myth of Prometheus in European literature over a broad chronological and linguistic range. These works continue to be useful for those interested in gaining an overview of the influence of Prometheus in European literature and thought. Others have tended to focus more narrowly on the mythic figure of Prometheus as he appears in the works of a single author or time period. Jean-Pierre Vernant's structural analysis of Prometheus in Hesiod, for example, demonstrates brilliantly how Prometheus' myth elaborates the cultural system of archaic Greece. Stuart Curran, Linda Lewis, and other scholars of the Romantic period have produced similarly insightful studies of Prometheus in the works of Shelley, Byron, and Goethe.

My goal here is to combine some of the historical range of the survey approach to the myth of Prometheus with the analytical intensity of the more narrowly focused studies. To this end, I have chosen several key historical moments when Prometheus was particularly influential and important. Within each chapter I have two methodological aims – first to isolate and explain how particular historical, cultural, and political circumstances inspire and generate specific readings of the Prometheus myth in the art and literature of that time. Second, I will elaborate those aspects of Prometheus that transcend time and place to define the human condition in more universal terms. To illuminate the sequence of historical readings most clearly, I have chosen to follow a generally chronological approach to the myth of Prometheus, although within the broadly chronological flow of the argument, my concentration on key themes and the importance of Prometheus for illuminating universal attributes of the human condition means that my analysis must be thematic rather than strictly historical.

The book begins with archaic Greece and the two poems of Hesiod that offer our earliest extended literary treatment of the myth. Hesiod's Prometheus is a trickster figure, responsible for the decline of the human experience from earlier days of ease and wealth. Two centuries later in the prosperous and powerful city of Athens, Prometheus tells a very different story of the human experience. Drawing on a range of literary, visual, and material evidence, the next two chapters will sketch out the ways that Prometheus as bringer of fire and technology figured in the political and cultural imaginary of classical Athens. The fourth chapter will show how the rebellious aspect of Prometheus – both in political and creative terms – captured the imagination of the Romantics, especially in England in the early decades of the nineteenth century. As much of the hopes, fears, and disappointments of the age focussed on the charismatic yet problematic figure of Napoleon, the rich ambiguity inherent in the mythical personal of Prometheus was especially useful for poets, novelists, and artists alike. The final chapter, then, will focus on the English poet Tony Harrison's 1998 film *Prometheus*, to learn how Prometheus, both as patron saint of technology and as the representative of the powerless worker, continues to structure our views of the human condition in the twentieth century and beyond. Harrison looks back to the mythic tradition of both Hesiod and Aeschylus through the lens of Shelley's *Prometheus Unbound* to offer a powerful critique of Prometheus' gifts to mankind, and in this respect his film will serve as the ideal text from which to draw some general conclusions about Prometheus' broader mythic significance.

The myth of Prometheus is infinitely expansive and flexible, and it will continue to adapt itself to different historical realities and circumstances as long as we wish to explore and challenge the limits and potential of the human experience. Now, as in the time of Hesiod, Aeschylus and the Romantics, the myth of Prometheus provides important opportunities for productive cultural thought and intro-spection.

KEY THEMES

I

THE TRICKSTER

Hesiod's Prometheus

The Greek historian Herodotus tells us that Homer and Hesiod were the poets who taught the Greeks about their gods: 'it is they who created for the Greeks their theogony, giving to the gods their special names, distributing their honors and their skills, and revealing their forms' (2.53.2). Although Homer makes no mention of Prometheus, Hesiod includes his story in two of the poems that are attributed to him, the *Theogony*, a poem about the origins of the gods and the world, and the *Works and Days*, a didactic poem in the tradition of wisdom literature. Taken together, Hesiod's poems offer the obvious point of departure for studies of Prometheus in the ancient world as well as his modern reception. They present Prometheus as a trickster figure and offer powerful testimony to the ways in which his myth helped the Greeks of the archaic period think about the nature of the human condition in all its complexity and ambiguity. Hesiod draws upon Prometheus' gift of fire to humans to mark the separation of mankind from the world of the gods and to explain the suffering and work that characterize the human experience at this time. Sandwiched between the rich palace world of the Homeric poems and the budding prosperity and innovation of the classical age, the world of Hesiod is one of scarce resources and limited opportunities. Hesiod uses Prometheus' battle of wits with Zeus – his theft of fire, the origins of sacrifice, Zeus' counter-gift of Pandora – to help Greeks of his time think about why their life is so difficult. Hesiod's Prometheus describes human existence as a decline from days of former wealth and ease. The introduction of Pandora, with her jar of evils and sickness, highlights the problematic role of women within the broader human experience as well. Before looking more closely at Hesiod's Prometheus, we need to get a better understanding of Hesiod – his works and his times.

HESIOD AND HIS TIMES

The poet whom we know as Hesiod tells us a fair amount about himself in his poems. In the *Works and Days*, for example, we learn that his father came from Kyme, a city on the coast of Asia Minor, from which he fled 'awful poverty' and took to sailing as a merchant, ending up in Askra, a village in western Boeotia, which Hesiod describes as 'bad in winter, godawful in summer, nice never' (*Works and Days* 640). Hesiod addresses the poem to his brother, Perses, inveighing upon him to stop his profligate ways and begging him to leave off from his lawsuits over their father's inheritance and to settle down to some productive work. And in the *Theogony*, Hesiod gives us his name and tells us that while tending his flocks upon the slopes of Mt Helikon, the Muses handed him a staff of laurel and inspired him with divine song so that he might celebrate past and future.

It is in large part because of these 'autobiographical' details that we tend to think of Hesiod and his poetry as something quite different from the anonymous bard of the Homeric poems. Hesiod, by contrast, brings a strong personal voice and personality to his poetry, creating the impression that he is singing about aspects of his own life. And yet, Hesiod's techniques of self-reference belong to traditions older than the poet himself. In each poem, he creates an authorial persona that straddles the divide between historical reality and poetic fiction in ways that can be frustrating to modern readers and scholars. In the *Theogony*, for example, Hesiod adopts the role of the encomiastic hymnic poet, while in the *Works and Days*, he combines what Richard Martin has called the authoritative voice of the outsider with the traditional role of dispenser of advice common to the genre of wisdom literature. Gregory Nagy has even suggested that the etymology of the name Hesiod means 'he who emits the voice', representing the poet not as an historical individual, but rather as a generic figure who embodies the singing power of the Muses.

The world that Hesiod describes in the *Works and Days*, characterized as it is by powerful, 'gift-devouring' kings and subsistence agriculture, corresponds to what little we know about the Greek world in the archaic period, the eighth to seventh centuries BC. Following the period known sometimes as the Dark Age, the archaic period is marked by increased contact between Greek cities and the larger Mediterranean world, in part through trade and in part through overseas colonization, and while this shift in economic orientation and scale brought increased prosperity to some, primarily the elite, the less well off, as we can see from Hesiod's *Works and Days*, experienced a decrease in opportunities and resources, left to fend for themselves in an increasingly unforgiving agricultural economy.

Taken together, the *Theogony* and the *Works and Days* offer us unique access to the Prometheus of the archaic period. His theft of fire for mankind and subsequent punishment at the hands of Zeus play an important role in both poems, and each time, the account is told slightly differently, influenced by the conventions of literary genre as well as by aspects of social and historical context. In spite of their differences, the two accounts complement each other and present a coherent portrait of Prometheus as a trickster figure symbolic of the human struggle to make the world habitable in the archaic period. In addition, the myth provides a commentary on the human condition in early archaic Greece.

The *Theogony* weaves together many disparate mythological strands to present a comprehensive poetic account of the origin of the universe structured as a genealogy and organized into successive generations. The *Works and Days*, on the other hand, is an example of a genre known as 'wisdom literature', characterized by advice about general conduct combined with truisms and general knowledge – all put into a largely fictitious setting. In each of these very different literary contexts, Hesiod draws upon the mythic figure of Prometheus. Although different aspects of the myth are highlighted or downplayed in each poem, the basic outline is the same. If we put the two together the story would go something like the following.

HESIOD'S PROMETHEUS

In the *Theogony*, Prometheus is the son of Iapetus the Titan and the Oceanid Klymene; he has three brothers, Menoitios, Atlas, and Epimetheus, all of whom have suffered at the hands of Zeus. As part of a bigger project to praise the rule of Zeus, Hesiod introduces Prometheus as one who dared to match wits with mighty Zeus but ultimately failed. He explains that when the gods and mortals were together at a place called Mekone, Prometheus butchered a big ox and divided up the victim for gods and men. He tricked Zeus into choosing the bones and fat, leaving the rich meat for humans to eat:

> This was Prometheus' trick. But Zeus, eternally wise,
> Recognized the fraud and began to rumble in his heart
> Trouble for mortals, and it would be fulfilled.
> With both his hands he picked up the gleaming fat.
> Anger seethed in his lungs and bile rose to his heart
> When he saw the ox's white bones artfully tricked out.
>
> *(Theogony 550–55)*

And that, Hesiod explains, is why at a sacrifice men offer the gods the inedible bones and fat and keep the more valuable cooked meat for themselves. Zeus, however, was furious at Prometheus' deception, and in return he withheld the 'power of weariless fire' from humans. Prometheus then stole fire back for mankind, hiding it in a hollow fennel stalk, and Zeus, when he saw fire burning again among men, retaliated by creating 'trouble to pay for fire': the first woman.

In the *Works and Days*, Hesiod gives this woman a name, Pandora, because 'all the Olympians donated something' to her creation. Hephaestus kneaded some earth and water and gave her a voice and a beautiful figure; Athena taught her embroidery and weaving; Aphrodite endowed her with grace and desire, and Hermes gave her a 'bitchy mind and a cheating heart'. When the gods were finished creating Pandora, Zeus sent Hermes to take her to Epimetheus, Prometheus' slow-witted brother, who accepted her on behalf of mankind, only remembering too late that his brother had warned him not to accept gifts from Zeus. And, as Hesiod observes, now, as a result, humans no longer live without trouble and work, for Pandora brought with her a large storage jar containing all the miseries and troubles that beset humankind which she scattered all over the earth. Only Hope was left in the jar, unable to fly out before Pandora slammed down the lid on her. As a result, Hesiod concludes, 'the earth is full of evil things and so's the sea'.

With Pandora and her jar of evils, Zeus brings suffering to mankind in retaliation for their enjoyment of fire, but for Prometheus he has another punishment:

> And he bound Prometheus with ineluctable fetters,
> Painful bonds, and drove a shaft through his middle,
> And set a long-winged eagle on him that kept gnawing
> His undying liver, but whatever the long-winged bird
> Ate the whole day through, would all grow back by night.
> That bird the mighty son of pretty-ankled Alkmene
> Herakles, killed, drove off the evil affliction
> From Iapetos' son and freed him from his misery.
>
> (*Theogony* 521–28)

And so, with this comparatively brief account of Zeus' punishment of the Titan and his eventual liberation at the hands of Heracles, Hesiod ends the story of Prometheus.

PROMETHEUS VS ZEUS: A BATTLE OF WITS

In the *Theogony*, the myth of Prometheus functions as part of the poet's broader strategy to celebrate Zeus' acquisition and consolidation of power. Hesiod tells us that in order to avoid the fate of the two previous generations, Zeus draws upon a combination of physical and intellectual skills to solidify his position as king of gods and men. When warned that he, like his father before him, would be overthrown by a son born to him from Metis, the personification of intellectual cleverness, Zeus swallowed her, effectively filling himself with her power. In Greek thought, the goddess Metis represents the kind of intellectual skill associated with trickery, deception, and lies; *metis* is often contrasted with strength or physical power and operates in shifting terrain and ambiguous settings. Nestor, for example, advises Antilochus in Book 23 of the *Iliad* that the charioteer triumphs over his rival through *metis* just as: 'It is through *metis* rather than through strength that the wood-cutter is much better. It is through *metis* moreover that the helmsman guides the swift ship upon the wine-dark sea against the wind, and it is by *metis* that charioteer excels charioteer' (*Iliad* 23. 315–18). The semantic field of *metis* also includes a kind of practical effectiveness, a resourcefulness of any kind whether it be the mastery of a craft, success in a particular activity or cunning strategy in war. Prometheus, too, the god whom Hesiod describes as 'capable of wriggling out of even the inextricable', is here presented as the very prototype of *metis* – his very name contains the word. Prometheus' anticipatory knowledge well equips him to duel with Zeus in wits.

Turning back to the *Theogony*, we see that the Prometheus story functions there to celebrate Zeus' intelligence. The episode opens and closes with reference to Zeus' punishment of Prometheus repeating the refrain 'no one can deceive Zeus, not even the very clever and tricky Prometheus'. The first thing we notice is the myth's focus on deception. Words for trickiness and cleverness are used fifteen times to describe the nature and actions of Prometheus and Zeus in this passage (535–616); in fact, the episode is structured as a contest in cleverness.

Round one: Prometheus tries to trick Zeus with the unequal sacrifice portions, but Zeus is not to be fooled. He replies:

> 'Iapetos' boy, if you're not the smartest of them all.
> So you still haven't forgotten your tricks, have you?'
> (*Theogony* 543–44)

But Zeus, the god 'whose wisdom never wears out', retaliates by withholding the power of fire from mortals. Round two: Prometheus outwits Zeus by stealing fire and hiding it in a fennel stalk to return it to mortals, but once Zeus sees 'the distant gleam of fire among men', he arranges for the creation of the first woman whom Hesiod characterizes as a 'sheer deception irresistible to men', thus outwitting the very clever Prometheus in the final round. Unlike Zeus' conquest of the monstrous Typhoeus or his fierce battle with the rest of the Titans, the competition between Prometheus and Zeus is one of intellectual prowess, not physical strength. In part, the myth of Prometheus is introduced in celebration of Zeus' own intellectual prowess – if Zeus can outwit Prometheus, he can outsmart anyone.

PROMETHEUS AS TRICKSTER

In this respect, Hesiod's Prometheus, his associations with cleverness, trickery, and deception, has much in common with the trickster figure that appears in the mythological and folklore traditions of nearly every traditional society – sometimes as a god, sometimes as an animal. Tricksters are ambiguous and anomalous figures; they are deceivers, even shape-shifters, and they often bridge the divine and mortal worlds. In an essay on the North American Indian trickster, Mac Linscott Ricketts defines a trickster as

the one who changes the chaotic myth-world into the ordered creation of today; he is the slayer of monsters, the thief of daylight, fire water, and the like for the benefit of man; he is the teacher of cultural skills and customs; but he is also a prankster who is grossly erotic, insatiably hungry, inordinately vain, deceitful, and cunning toward friends as well as foes; a restless wanderer upon the face of the earth and a blunderer who is often the victim of his own tricks and follies.

(Ricketts 1965: 327)

Two of the best-known trickster figures are the Native American Coyote and Anansi the spider-trickster from West Africa. Each delights his own people with his antics, and yet his irreverence calls the ordinary categories of daily life into question. Tricksters speak the truth through deception, and for this reason, trickster tales are more than a source of amusement and play. They are deeply embedded in the social experience of those who tell them.

Trickster figures are often associated with theft and deception rather than with the use of force or violence, and Hesiod's Prometheus certainly fits this description. Norman O. Brown has pointed out that the Greek verb usually translated as 'to steal' (*kleptein*) really means to remove secretly, to deceive, or to use secret action, and Hesiod's Prometheus unites both these senses when he steals fire from the heavens by hiding it in a fennel stalk. For all their cleverness and wit, tricksters are also often portrayed as dull-witted, responsible for disorder or chaos. In the trickster narrative, cunning and stupidity go together, each one illuminating the other, and Carl Kerényi has observed that the positive and the negative qualities of the traditional trickster figure are expressed in the Greek tradition through the two brothers Prometheus and Epimetheus:

> Every invention of Prometheus brings new misery upon mankind. No sooner has he succeeded in offering sacrifice than Zeus deprives mankind of the fire. And when, after stealing the fire, Prometheus himself is snatched away from mortals to suffer punishment, Epimetheus is left behind as their representative: craftiness is replaced by stupidity. The profound affinity between these two figures is expressed in the fact that they are brothers. One might almost say that in them a single primitive being, sly and stupid at once, has been split into a duality: Prometheus the Forethinker, Epimetheus the belated Afterthinker. It is he who in his thoughtlessness, brings mankind, as a gift from the gods, the final inexhaustible source of misery: Pandora.
>
> (Kerényi in Radin 1956: 181)

For all his efforts and cleverness, Hesiod's Prometheus does not actually help mankind through his deceptions of Zeus (sacrifice, fire). Not only is he himself punished for the theft, but Prometheus is directly responsible for human suffering and for the separation of mankind from the ease of the divine world.

In this respect, Prometheus' tale, like that of other trickster figures, establishes the human world 'as it is' – not as it should be. And he does so, in spite of, not in accordance with, the plans of the gods. Tricksters often appear as transformational figures; they embody the human struggle to make the world more human. Trickster tales help probe a culture's inner workings, for nothing confirms the meaning of social order more impressively than recognition of that which evades order. Moving fluidly across boundaries – above/below, male/female, nature/culture – the ambiguous figure of the trickster represents man himself in a liminal state and celebrates the creative and transformational power of that liminal state.

The complexity of trickster figures, whether that of the west African Anansi or the archaic Greek Prometheus, is best appreciated by keeping him firmly within his own cultural context, and doing so can also reveal a great deal about that culture. In the case of Prometheus, a divine figure whose theft of fire upset the world of gods and men alike, his actions both threaten and reaffirm the rules and conventions that constitute archaic Greek culture. In particular, Prometheus' story calls attention to important cultural divisions and boundaries of archaic Greece – the boundaries between humans and gods, between humans and beasts, between men and women. In addition, it accounts for those human institutions that defined Greek life at that time: sacrifice, marriage, agriculture. And finally, its focus on hiding, deception, and trickery represents the ambiguous nature of the human condition as the Greeks conceived it.

PROMETHEUS AND THE HUMAN CONDITION

In an influential essay, 'The Myth of Prometheus in Hesiod', the French classicist Jean-Pierre Vernant argues that Prometheus' story 'defines the status of man, midway between that of the beasts and that of the gods: It is characterized by sacrifice, fire for culinary and technical operations, the woman seen both as a wife and as a bestial stomach, and cereal foods and agricultural labor' (Vernant 1988: 192). In addition, he notes that the trick of Prometheus, his theft of fire, consecrates the separation of men and gods through the institution of sacrifice, and it does so with inevitable consequences: (stolen) fire, woman and marriage, agriculture and work. Finally, these elements are all inextricably embedded in the core of the myth. Hesiod's two tellings of the Prometheus myth have a certain complementary logic, and they can provide valuable insight into the ways in which Prometheus the trickster helped establish the human condition in archaic Greece.

Sacrifice

In addition to consecrating Zeus' position as the ruling god among gods, the Prometheus myth in the *Theogony* addresses relations between the divine and mortal worlds. In particular, Prometheus' theft of fire for mankind is linked to the first sacrifice at Mekone, the moment that marks the initial separation of gods and men. It all happened, Hesiod tells us, when 'gods and mortal men were negotiating at Mekone'. According to Callimachus and others, Mekone is the place where the gods established their seat and divided up their privileges at the end of the war against the Giants. As both an earthly site and an abode for the gods, it comes to represent a place where men and gods can live side by side, feasting at the same tables and eating the same food. Mekone is also the ancient name for Sicyon, and between Sicyon and Corinth lay an extremely rich plain whose reputation for fertility was proverbial – to become rich, all you had to do was to own land between Sicyon and Corinth! And so in addition to recalling a memory of gods and men living side by side, Mekone evokes the image of bountiful plenty, a golden-age world of effortless plentitude and fertility. And it is at this Mekone that Hesiod tells us that gods and men were negotiating when Prometheus butchered a great ox and divided it up in an attempt to deceive Zeus. He made two unequal portions:

> For Zeus he set out flesh and innards rich with fat
> Laid out on the oxhide and covered with its paunch.
> But for the others he set out the animal's white bones
> Artfully dressed out and covered with shining fat.
>
> (*Theogony* 538–41)

When Zeus chooses the bones covered deceptively with shining fat, the myth provides an *aition*, or explanation, for the great paradox posed by the institution of sacrifice. If the sacrificial killing and cooking of an animal is an offering to the gods intended to honour them and to encourage their favour, why do men keep the best portions for themselves? That the myth of Prometheus offers a culturally satisfying solution to this dilemma is important, for the Greeks only ate meat that came from ritually slaughtered animals.

While Prometheus' sacrifice at Mekone marks the initial separation of gods and men, sacrifice as practised within the Greek city extends this principle of division to reinforce social and political relationships within the human community as well. All military and political undertakings – the conclusion of treaties, the opening of the assembly, the assumption of political office – demanded a sacrifice, and the distribution of sacrificial portions to members of the city reflects and enacts political participation and power. Blood sacrifice, then, plays a central role in Greek religious and political thought, and thanks to Prometheus, communication between men and gods is made possible by a religious and political institution whose tale of origin articulates the insurmountable distance between them.

Work

Even though it is a poem of origins, the *Theogony* does not concern itself with the actual creation of mankind. Prometheus' actions in the poem do not bring men into existence; instead, they define the nature and terms of the mortal condition by contrast with the eternal and blissful state of the gods. In the *Works and Days*, Hesiod pairs the Prometheus story with a tale of the five ages of mankind – a mythic account of the decline of the human experience from the days of the Golden Age when men lived like gods to the present-day challenges of the Iron Age when 'not a day goes by a man doesn't have some kind of trouble'. In this context, Promethean trickery generates an explanation for why, after Mekone, men must always work for their food.

According to Hesiod, Prometheus' attempt to deceive Zeus with the sacrificial distribution at Mekone sets up a chain of events that leads inexorably towards a lifetime of toil and trouble for mankind. In the *Works and Days*, Hesiod introduces the story of Prometheus neither as an explanation for Zeus' authority or intelligence, nor as the origins of sacrifice, but to account for the inescapable fact that humans must work – it is all thanks to Prometheus:

> You know, the gods never have let on
> How humans might make a living. Else,

> You might get enough done in one day
> To keep you fixed for a year without working.
> You might just hang your plowshare up in the smoke,
> And all the fieldwork done by your oxen
> And hard-working mules would soon run to ruin.
> But Zeus got his spleen up, and went and hid
> How to make a living, all because shifty Prometheus
> Tricked him. That's why Zeus made life hard for humans.
>
> *(Works and Days* 42–49)

When Prometheus stole fire back for mankind, Zeus next sent Pandora as 'an evil in exchange for fire, their very own evil to love and embrace'. Whereas previously, Hesiod explains to his brother Perses, men lived in a world free of daily toil and disease, now, thanks to the arrival of Pandora and her jar of evils, the world is a much harder place for mortals:

> Because before that the human race
> Had lived off the land without any trouble, no hard work,
> No sickness or pain that the Fates give to men
> (And when men are in misery they show their age quickly).
> But the woman took the lid off the big jar with her hands
> And scattered all the miseries that spell sorrow for men.
>
> *(Works and Days* 90–95)

This time, the story starts with Zeus' anger at being tricked by Prometheus at the first sacrifice and introduces work and women as the two-pronged consequences of that trick. Previously, the earth gave its produce freely to mankind, but now Zeus has hidden man's means of livelihood (*bios*) in addition to witholding fire. In other words, now humans must work the land – plough, sow, reap – in order to take advantage of its fruit or grain. And so it is the human institution of agriculture rather than sacrifice that is emphasized here. A poem in celebration of work, the *Works and Days* defines mortal existence in archaic Greece in terms of hard manual labour, especially by contrast with the carefree existence of the gods. In this context, the story of Prometheus' actions, together with the myth of the five ages, articulates the origins of this basic fact – humans must work for their livelihood but the gods do not.

Hesiod's poems use the Prometheus myth first to narrate mankind's separation from the gods and then to examine its consequences. While the *Theogony* highlights the first sacrifice as the impetus for the break, the *Works and Days* elaborates the emergence and necessity of work, especially agricultural work, that follows from it. In a post-Golden Age world, men must work to get grain and fruit from the earth. At the other end of the spectrum, as well, Prometheus patrols the boundaries between men and beasts. Men domesticate animals to work the land and kill them in a ritual for the gods, and sacrifice and agriculture emerge from Prometheus' myth as two institutions that draw the line between man and animals. The story of Prometheus thus charts out a space for humans between the carefree gods, on the one hand, and beasts of burden or sacrificial animals, on the other. Not only does Hesiod's Prometheus characterize the human condition in terms of these key social institutions, two specific elements of the myth – fire and Pandora – emphasize the tentative and ambiguous nature of this human experience, founded as it was in deception and trickery and located in a problematic intermediary location between gods and beasts.

Pandora

Within the logic of the myth the figure of Pandora functions to highlight the interconnectedness of those institutions that define the human condition. The creation of Pandora at the end of the story in the *Works and Days*, for example, recalls the shares of the first sacrifice described at the beginning of the *Theogony* version. Like the portion that Prometheus offers to Zeus, Pandora is beautiful on the outside, and yet her beauty hides a mean and deceptive interior. At the same time Pandora's role in the myth corresponds to Promethean fire in the myth. She was created in exchange for fire and, like it, she is always hungry, always in need of being fed, her thieving nature echoing the original theft of fire that led to her creation. The myth uses the theme of hunger to establish links between Pandora and agriculture too. In addition to its need to be fed, the belly of woman, like the earth, can produce life – the seeds of man and grain alike must be hidden within them to prosper.

Within Hesiod's telling of the Prometheus myth, Pandora's deceptive and dual nature serves as a symbol, then, of the fundamental ambiguity of human existence. A product of the deception and trickery of the gods, Pandora combines all the tensions and ambiguities that characterize the status of humankind. Through the charm and beauty of her external appearance, she participates in the world of the gods, yet through the meanness of her inner nature, she belongs to the world of the beasts. She is both part of mankind and yet the progenitor of a race apart, the race of women. She brings with her Hope, which like strife, can take both positive and negative forms: it can encourage a man to work hard to fill his storage jar with grain in anticipation of a prosperous future or it can delude an idle man into an unrealistic expectation of a life of ease. Neither gods nor beasts have any need for hope, only humans who are defined by their curiosity about the future together with their imperfect knowledge of it.

Moreover, Hesiod's treatment of the Prometheus myth makes it very clear that gender issues are very much at the heart of the human condition in archaic Greece. The misogyny inherent in Hesiod's story of Prometheus and Pandora is difficult to overlook, and we can locate Pandora's story within a larger, cross-cultural tradition that creates women as secondary to men and associates her creation with all the negative aspects of the human experience: death, sickness, work. There are obvious parallels between Pandora's creation and the tradition of Adam and Eve, for example, in *Genesis*. The forbidden fruit that the serpent persuades Eve to eat confers knowledge of both good and evil. It both brings the enlightenment that makes civilization possible and it severs the human bond with nature, and in this respect corresponds to Promethean fire.

Still, even within this broader tradition, the misogyny of Hesiod's version is particularly virulent. Pandora, after all, is not created as a companion for man, as Eve is for Adam (Genesis 2.21) but rather as a punishment. Nor is there any reconciliation between men and women after the fact; instead, Hesiod outlines a stark asymmetry of labour in which men work all the time and women are idle. Hesiod fails to include any of the many ways in which women can and do contribute to a household – neither the childbearing, weaving, or other work often done by women. In their place, he highlights the dangers of female sexuality, suppressing all positive connections with fertility. He reverses the traditional etymology of Pandora's name, usually associated with the generosity of Mother Earth as 'giver of all' to make her instead the passive recipient of the gifts of the gods. Hesiod's Pandora is a taker rather than a giver.

It is also significant that Pandora brings with her a jar – not a box – of evils. The familiar term 'Pandora's box' can be traced back to the Renaissance scholar Erasmus of Rotterdam (1508), who probably confused Pandora's large storage jar (*pithos*) with the more delicate box (*pyxis*) that Psyche opens against instructions in the Cupid and Psyche episode of Apuleius' *Golden Ass*. It is important to note this difference, not just for the sake of mythological pedantry, but because this large storage jar was of the kind typically used to store grain or olive oil and thus takes us back to the theme of agriculture and the post-Promethean need for humans to store food from harvest to harvest; no longer does the earth give food freely without season. Second, Pandora's *pithos* is the kind of jar that we find invoked in the Hippocratic corpus and other medical writings as an image of a woman's uterus. Women's bodies were often characterized as vessels or containers, and Pandora's jar thus brings the anxiety about having sufficient food and resources together with concerns about female sexuality and the appropriate number and value of children in times of scarce resources.

While the misogynistic aspects of Hesiod's mythic tradition about Prometheus and Pandora can be explained to some extent by the historical, economic, and social constraints of the time, it is also true that these myths continue to be told and retold once they are embedded in important and influential literary texts, providing a kind of timeless authority for their views. In this way we can see just how powerful a role myths and mythmaking can play in the construction of gender – Hesiod's story of the creation of woman as a curse for mankind, as a punishment, a source of evil and unrelenting work, does more than justify the gender inequalities of Hesiod's world. It 'naturalizes' in Barthes' sense, the social construction of men and women in a broader cultural context as well (Barthes 1972: 142).

Not only do men no longer eat together with the gods, thanks to Prometheus, but they also must live with women. Hesiod introduces Prometheus' theft of fire as both the consequence of the institution of sacrifice and as the catalyst for the creation of woman, whom Zeus ordered as 'trouble to pay for the fire'. The craftsman Hephaestus, with the help of the other gods, is ordered to mould some clay to look 'like a shy virgin'. She is 'intricately designed and a wonder to look at', and Hesiod explains that she is 'sheer deception, irresistible to men'. From her comes first 'the deadly race and population of female women' and second, the problematic institution of marriage, 'another evil/ to offset the good'. Hesiod goes on to explain that the unmarried man lives to an old age but dies with no sons to support him or to inherit his estate while the married man, even if he marries a good wife, has a life 'balanced between evil and good, a constant struggle'. Life with women is at best, then, a mixed proposition, and in this respect, Pandora's jar also recalls Zeus' twin jars of good and evil in the *Iliad* – as a human, the most one can hope for is a life of good and evil mixed.

Hope

In the *Works and Days*, not only is Pandora named, but she introduces Prometheus' slow-thinking brother Epimetheus into the story – he is the one who receives the gift from Zeus – and she brings with her a jar filled with all the troubles and sickness in the world. In this respect, the *Works and Days* introduces a new element to the Prometheus story – mankind's partial and problematic knowledge of the future. The significance of Prometheus' name – its etymology as 'forethought' – is highlighted in this version thanks to the introduction of his brother, Epimetheus, whose name means 'afterthought' and whose actions fulfil its etymology. Prometheus had warned his brother not to accept any gifts from Zeus, fearing (correctly) some act of retribution against mortals, but Epimetheus did not remember the warning until it was too late and he had accepted the gift of Pandora. She brings with her, of course, a jar full of trouble and Hope:

But the woman took the lid off the big jar with her hands
And scattered all the miseries that spell sorrow for men.
Only Hope was left there in the unbreakable container,
Stuck under the lip of the jar, and couldn't fly out:
The woman clamped the lid back on the jar first.

(Works and Days 94–98)

Hope appears to have been inside Pandora's jar together with all the unspeakable ills that now torment mankind. Whereas the *Theogony* invokes Prometheus' cleverness to emphasize Zeus' supreme knowledge and intelligence, the *Works and Days* takes Prometheus' myth in a different direction. Both the etymology of his name – forethought – and the introduction of Hope into Prometheus' story emphasize the theme of man's imperfect knowledge of the future – another characteristic of the human condition. While the gods know all things and have all things, humans do not; humans have only hope or expectations to guide their choices about the future.

Furthermore, by contrast with our modern optimistic notion, hope in the archaic world was a much dicier proposition, and it is hard to know just how to read this passage. When Pandora traps Hope in the jar does that mean that Hope is all that is left for mankind, a mechanism for coping with the difficulties and trials of human existence? Or is Hope not available for mortals – its absence just one more aspect of a dim and dismal world-view? The logic of Hesiod's myth is ambiguous: hope is both bad by virtue of its association with all the other evils in Pandora's jar and good in that it alone was not released. At best, then, like Pandora, hope is a mixed blessing. Other Greek poets confirm the duality of the nature of hope. Both Semonides and Solon emphasize the deceptive nature of hope, distracting men from the hard facts of reality while Theognis offers a more optimistic reading: 'Hope is the only good god that remains for mankind;/ all the others have left and gone to Olympus' (1135–36). Hope can derail productive human activity, or it can refer more positively to one's expectations of the future, and Hesiod's version keeps both these attitudes in the picture. At the very least, Hesiod's ambivalent image here raises interesting questions about the nature of hope and its presence in human lives.

What emerges from our reading of Hesiod's myth of Prometheus, then, is a commentary on the nature and status of the human condition in archaic Greece – as it is, not as it should be. As a consequence of Prometheus' actions humans live on earth with countless troubles; they eat grain that they have worked; they eat meat that is cooked, they live together with women, and they can only communicate with gods through sacrifice. While Hesiod's Prometheus does not actually create mankind from clay, he is directly responsible for the three inseparable aspects of what it means to be human in archaic Greece – sacrifice, marriage, and agriculture.

OVERVIEW

In the archaic world of Hesiod, Prometheus figures as a trickster, an advocate for mankind whose efforts on their behalf contribute to their initial separation from the gods and the ensuing difficulties and challenges that mark the human condition. Hesiod's Prometheus' tale locates mortals somewhere between the realm of the gods and that of beasts in a world defined by the institutions of sacrifice, agriculture, marriage, and an imperfect knowledge of the future – all of which are linked within the logic of the myth to Prometheus' theft of fire and the creation of Pandora. In addition, the prominent position that Hesiod gives Pandora and her jar of evils in the Prometheus myth suggests that sexuality and gender relations played an important role in thinking about the nature of the human condition at this time. Reading Hesiod's Prometheus within the cross-cultural context of trickster tales, we can recognize the way in which his myth helps probe the inner workings of archaic Greek culture. The ambiguity at the heart of his story here articulates the necessary connections between the cultural categories of mortal and divine, human and animal, male and female, culture and nature. Moreover, the trickster status of Prometheus – god who steals fire for mortals and is punished for it – helps generate a compelling narrative of human experience as it was in archaic Greece: a patriarchal, agricultural society living in times of scarce resources.

Whereas later traditions, even Greek ones, characterize Prometheus' gift of fire to mankind as the moment from which human progress begins, Hesiod focuses on the other end of the spectrum and reads the myth as a fall from the Golden Age. The actions of his Prometheus, the invention of sacrifice and the subsequent theft of fire, mark the moment when humans first broke with the gods, and life has been a struggle ever since.

2

THE CULT OF
PROMETHEUS AT ATHENS

In spite of his prominence in Hesiod and other writers, Prometheus seems to have played a minor role in the religious life of archaic and classical Greeks – a fact that the second sophistic writer, Lucian of Samosata (c. AD 120–80), pokes fun at in a piece entitled 'Prometheus'. Written as a parody of the opening scene of Aeschylus' *Prometheus Bound*, the dialogue is set in the Caucasus where Hermes and Hephaestus prepare to nail Prometheus to the mountain. Structured as a kind of trial, the dialogue has Hermes and Hephaestus offer the case against the god who stole fire and created mortals while Prometheus is left to defend himself. He points out that none of the other gods have actually suffered through his actions, but rather have benefited a great deal. Thanks to Prometheus' gifts, the entire earth is adorned with cities and cultivation, the sea is sailed, and everywhere there are altars, sacrifices, temples, and festivals. In fact, he concludes, 'there are temples to Zeus, to Apollo, to Hera and to you, Hermes, everywhere in sight, but nowhere any to Prometheus' (Lucian, *Prometheus* 14).

Although, as Lucian's dialogue suggests, Prometheus may have been neglected in other cities, in Athens, it was a very different story. The city of Athens celebrated Prometheus, linking him in myth and ritual with both Athena and Hephaestus, and in this chapter we will discuss the cult of Prometheus in Athens, highlighting his association with fire in all its beneficial and destructive aspects. The Athenians erected an altar to Prometheus in the Academy, which provided the starting place for several important processions and events in the Athenian civic calendar. The Panathenaic festival, for example, perhaps Athens' most significant civic festival, included a torch race that moved from the altar of Prometheus located outside the city proper, up to the city centre to light the sacrificial fire that concluded the festival. This chapter will sketch out some of the ways in which Prometheus as bringer of fire and technology figured in the religious and civic life of the Athenians. What is the nature of Prometheus' cult in Athens? How is it observed? What does it tell us about Prometheus? And about Athens?

In the previous chapter, we saw how the archaic poet Hesiod tells the story of Prometheus, the god who tricks Zeus, and shapes the account of his theft of fire within the familiar pattern of the trickster tale. In his role as trickster, Prometheus' story operates at the boundaries of human culture to define human experience in archaic Greece in terms of certain key institutions (sacrifice, agriculture, marriage). Of all human inventions, the ability to make and control fire – what Rudyard Kipling called 'man's red flower' – is no doubt one of the most significant, and this chapter will focus on the ways that Prometheus' gift of fire forms the basis for his worship and celebration in Athens. While other cities and other traditions associated different figures with the origins of fire – the Argives attributed its discovery to their ancient king Phoroneus (Paus. 2.19.5) and the *Homeric Hymn to Hermes* credits that god with rubbing dry sticks together to produce sparks – in Athens, Prometheus is responsible for bringing fire to mortals, and it is his association with fire that explains most of what we know about the ritual celebration of Prometheus.

FIRE IN GREEK CULTURE

Fire is the foundation of civilized life – it provides mankind with the technology to provide warmth, light, and protection from enemies and the elements – and yet it also can be the source of its total destruction. Even the strongest, most technologically advanced, man-made structures can be reduced to nothing but smoke and ashes by the power of fire. As Theophrastus explains in his treatise on fire (*De igne*), 'of the simple substances fire has the most special powers'. And so fire plays a part in almost every religious act of the Greeks – it kindles the flame burning at a god's altar, it lights the funeral pyre in a human burial as well as the torch that illuminates many nocturnal festivals and mystery cults. The heart of a religious sanctuary is its altar, and its ever-burning flame offers tangible proof of the god's continual presence. At the same time, the potential destructive power of fire provides a constant reminder of the capriciousness of divine will. Fire burning in the household centre embodies continuity in the human sphere as well. Hestia is the goddess of the family hearth, a symbol of the continuity and identity of the household across both generational and geographical boundaries. A lighted torch accompanied a young bride, bringing fire from her father's hearth to light that of her new husband. Similarly, but on a much larger scale, a flame from the civic centre of the mother-city accompanied those settlers embarking on a colonial expedition and would, eventually, light the first fire of the new civic foundation. The continuity of fire provided a symbolic connection between two households or two cities and, except in times of crisis, neither in homes nor shrines was the fire allowed to die.

At significant moments, however, the deliberate extinction and rekindling of fire symbolized purification and a new beginning. In Argos, when a family member died, the hearth-fire was extinguished and then relit. In Lemnos, at a certain time of year, all fire on the island was extinguished for a period of nine days until a sacred ship brought back new fire from the island of Delos. After the battle of Plataea, Plutarch tells us that the Greeks extinguished fires throughout the land so that they could be rekindled from the sacred fire at Delphi. The Greek commanders went about and forced all who were using fire to extinguish it. Meanwhile, a man named Euchidas was sent from Plataea to Delphi with all possible speed to bring the new purified fire back. Once he took the fire from the altar at Delphi, he started to run back to Plataea and got there before the sun had set, accomplishing the entire round trip in just one day. He greeted his fellow countrymen, handed them the fire, and died on the spot (*Aristides* 20). The story underscores the ritual significance of fire as symbolic of a city's survival in a time of crisis, and some scholars have suggested that this practice gives us a framework for interpreting the torch race as well – as a ritual reenactment of the need, in times of crisis, to rekindle a city's sacred fire.

The Pre-Socratic philosopher Heraclitus observed that 'All things are an equal exchange for fire and fire for all things, just as goods are for gold and gold for goods' (DK22B90). This notion of fire as the ultimate exchange mechanism is particularly indicative of the reciprocal relationship between gods and men. In spite of its key role in the religious practices of Greeks, fire itself never became a god nor the primary focus of worship, as it did in other traditions. Instead, as we have already seen from Hesiod's treatment of Prometheus' myth, fire functions as the key medium for communication between the divine and human worlds. Thanks to Prometheus' trick at Mekone, fire transfers men's gifts to the gods through sacrifice, and it is this same fire, stolen from Zeus, that cooks their meals. In other words, like Prometheus himself, rituals involving fire, especially sacrifice, enable a two-way communication between gods and men even as they reinforce their separate worlds.

Fire – a powerful symbol of divine presence, a source of both protection and devastation, the medium for contact and communication with the gods – is what Greek myth tells us that Prometheus brought to mankind in general. Now let us look more closely at the qualities, contexts, and uses of the fire that the Athenians say that Prometheus brought right into the city of fifth-century Athens itself.

PROMETHEUS IN ATHENIAN MYTH

First, it is important to note the ways that Prometheus is celebrated in Athens through his mythic connections with the city's patron goddess, Athena. As we saw in the previous chapter, Prometheus is famous for his *metis*, the same kind of cunning intelligence for which Athena is celebrated. The association is a fundamental one for both gods: Prometheus' very name contains the root *metis* while Athena was born from the head of Zeus after he swallowed the goddess Metis (a story told in Hesiod's *Theogony* and engraved in marble by Pheidias upon the east pediment of the Parthenon). This association is made even more explicit in a play of Euripides where Prometheus, not

Hephaestus, assisted with the axe at Athena's birth (Eur. *Ion* 455). Similarly, a variant on the Athenian myth of the birth of Erichthonius claims that it was Prometheus (not Hephaestus) who lusted after Athena, spilling on the ground the sperm from which Erichthonius was born, thus linking Prometheus with one of the most creative myths of Athenian civic identity (Duris FGH 76 F 47). For the story of Erichthonius' birth is a brilliant example of the Athenian mythopoetic process – merging the city's allegiance to Athena with its more recent autochthonous identity, and it is all the more significant that Prometheus is brought in as the creative force in that effort. Cleverness and intelligence are qualities that Athenians liked to attribute to themselves, and the appearance of Prometheus in key Athenian myths helps articulate that self-representation.

Not only do these mythic variants underscore Prometheus' connections with Athena, celebrating the clever intelligence they both share, they also suggest that Prometheus' mythic and cultic profile in Athens overlaps a great deal with that of the other Olympian god associated with fire and technology, Hephaestus. Both gods are associated with fire, metalwork, and crafts, and both are credited with the creation of humans. According to Lucian, Prometheus is worshipped as a potter in Athens, a fellow craftsman with Athena, and other traditions have Prometheus mould humans out of clay, much as Hephaestus made Pandora in Hesiod's *Works and Days*. According to one tradition that again links Athena with Prometheus, while Prometheus created mankind from clay, Athena helped him get the fire that would animate their minds, scaling the heights of Olympus to light the torch from the wheels of Helios' chariot (Servius' commentary on Vergil *Eclogues* 6.42).

PROMETHEUS IN CULT

Athena, Hephaestus, and Prometheus are brought together in Athens through cult as well as myth. All three gods are celebrated with festivals that include torch races, and Hephaestus and Prometheus are said to share an altar in the precinct of Athena in the Academy. Originally a sacred grove and perhaps most famous as the site of Plato's philosophical school, the Academy functioned primarily as a gymnasium in classical times. The area, said to derive its name from the hero Academus or Hecademus, lay outside the city to the northwest. A broad street, lined with tombs, led to it from the Dipylon Gate, about 2.5 kilometres from the city walls (Fig. 3). While several stretches of the aqueduct leading water to the groves of the Academy have been excavated, the Academy itself lies under the modern city and not much is known of the buildings themselves. What little we do know comes from later sources. The second-century AD Greek travel writer Pausanias, for example, has provided us with a general outline of the area. The tenth-century lexicon known as the Suda tells us that in the sixth century BC, Hipparchus, brother of the tyrant Hippias, built a wall around it at great public expense, and Plutarch, a Greek philosopher and antiquarian writer (AD 50–120), explains that Cimon first converted the area from a dry and dusty locale to a well-watered grove with shady walks as part of his larger project of rebuilding public buildings (*Cimon* 13).

The main precinct of the Academy belonged to Athena. An ancient commentator to Sophocles' tragedy *Oedipus at Colonus* tells us that in the Academy there was an old building with an altar where Prometheus, Hephaestus, and Athena were all worshipped in common. Near the entrance to this building was a pedestal on which Prometheus and Hephaestus were represented in bas-relief. Prometheus is portrayed there as an old man with a sceptre in his right hand while Hephaestus is shown as a youth in the secondary position. The altar captures the important relationship between these two fire gods, establishing Prometheus as the first and more senior of the two.

Perhaps most significantly, Prometheus, Athena, and Hephaestus were all linked in Athens through a common ritual activity. All three deities are associated with fire and its attendant technology, and a recognition of the significance of fire for human culture forms the basis for their celebration in the city of Athens. In the *Oedipus at Colonus*, Sophocles gives Prometheus the epithet *Purphoros*, 'bearer of fire', and Euripides, too, uses this adjective to describe the figure of Prometheus emblazoned on the torch of Capaneus in the *Phoenician Women* (1121–22). The adjective *purphoros* typically describes the thunderbolt of Zeus, and when applied to the human realm, it usually alludes

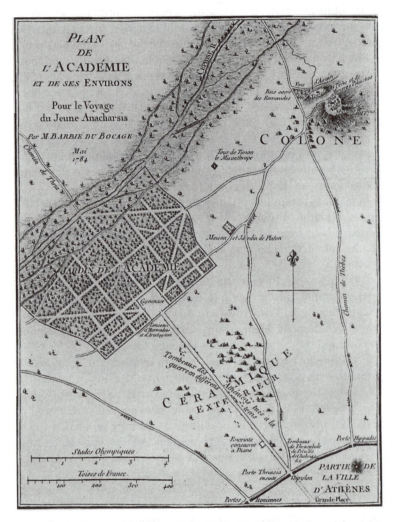

Figure 3 The Academy. Restored plan by M. Barbié du Bocage, *Recueil de cartes géographiques de l'ancienne Grèce*, 1790

Source: Photo from John Travlos, *The Pictorial Dictionary of Ancient Athens*, New York: Praeger, 45

to torches carried by Demeter, Persephone, or their votaries at the Mysteries of Eleusis. *Purphuros* thus describes Prometheus in a familiar aspect to Athenians as Fire-bearer, as one of three gods who taught the use of fire to mankind and who are honoured by torch festivals and worshipped in the Academy.

TORCH RACE

For the Greeks in general, the torch race (*lampas*) originated to celebrate Prometheus' gift of fire to mankind – to illustrate the civilizing element of fire as well as to commemorate the course that Prometheus once took from heaven to earth when he first brought fire to mankind. Certainly in Athens, the torch race is closely connected with the worship of Prometheus and his fellow fire gods. As we have seen in Hesiod, in earlier myth and legend Prometheus is known as the one who steals fire for mortals in a fennel stalk, but it is not until the fifth century that he becomes associated with the torch, and his famous theft serves as the mythic prototype of the Athenian torch races.

Pausanias describes the torch race and its course as follows:

> In the Academy there is an altar of Prometheus, and they run from it towards the city holding burning torches. The contest is both running and keeping the torch burning at the same time. If the torch of the first runner goes out, he no longer has the victory, but it belongs to the second runner in his place; but if he too allows his torch to go out, the third runner is the winner, and if everyone's torch is extinguished, no one gains the victory.

(Pausanias 1.30.2)

The race course for the Prometheia most probably started from the altar of Prometheus in the Academy and ran through the Kerameikos to the Dipylon Gate, or 'to the city', as Pausanias says, a distance of approximately three-quarters of a mile. One scholar argues that ending the torch race in the Prometheia at the threshold of the city, rather than within the city itself, symbolizes the original arrival of fire to mankind whereas festivals in honour of other gods celebrated the uses of fire.

Another suggests that the torch races in the Prometheia served to replenish the civic fire at the Prytaneum before the phratry celebration of the Apatouria where lighted torches were brought from the civic hearth to individual altars. Torch races run in honour of other gods may have started from Prometheus' altar or the nearby altar of Eros and gone further into the city, or perhaps, as in the case of the Panathenaea, to the altar of Athena where scholars have proposed that the flame was used to light the great sacrifice that marked the culmination of the festival.

In the *Frogs*, Aristophanes gives a humorous account of the torch race at the Panathenaea. The god Dionysus, who has descended to the underworld in search of a playwright, speaks with the deceased poet, Aeschylus, who in turn laments the current lack of training and discipline in Athens – no one has enough athletic training to run the torch race! – to which Dionysus responds:

> Amen to that! I about died laughing at the Panathenaea when some laggard was running, all pale-raced, stooped over, and fat, falling behind and struggling badly; and then at the Gates the Potter's Field people whacked his stomach, ribs flanks, and butt, and at their flat-handed slaps he started farting, and ran away blowing on his torch!
>
> (*Frogs* 1089–98; trans. Jeffery Henderson)

Apparently it was the custom of those living in the Kerameikos to treat slow runners in this fashion, producing the proverbial phrase: 'the Kerameikan slap'.

While Pausanias' account of the torch race describes a race of individual runners, each covering the entire length of the course holding his torch, other accounts suggest that the race was run by teams of relay runners. Herodotus, for example (8.98), compares the Persian postal messengers, who work as a relay team passing the message from station to station, to the Greek torch race. Similarly, Aeschylus likens the movement of the fire signals from Troy to Mycenae in Clytamnestra's famous beacon speech to a torch race: 'Such are the torch-bearers I have arranged. In succession one to the other, completing the course; and victor is he who ran both first and last' (*Agamemnon* 312–14). In fact, the running of torch races as a relay appears to be common to many traditions across cultures. In his collection of traditions about fire, Sir James Frazer explains that the Navaho people of New Mexico, for example, tell a story about animals running a sort of relay, each one handing the fire to another, to bring fire to mankind. Originally animals had fire, but men did not, and the coyote decided to steal some for mankind. He grabbed some fiery embers and ran off with them, pursued by all the other animals. When he grew tired, he passed the fire to the bat, who then handed it off to the squirrel, who managed to carry the fire safely to the Navaho people (Frazer 1930). The running of torch races as relays enables the runners to cover more distance with greater speed than any one individual could, no matter how fast, and may reflect the original use of the torch race to replenish a fire that has died out or become polluted.

In fifth-century Athens, a relay torch race organized by tribes would link the ritual to the major mechanism for the formation and maintenance of political identity in fifth-century Athens. A key component of the political reforms instituted by Cleisthenes in 508 BC was his decision to replace the four Ionian tribes that had previously dominated Athenian political life with ten new tribes named after autochthonous Athenian heroes. The formation of these tribes was based on geography, drawing citizens from different parts of the city together in one tribe, and these tribes served as the key means of organizing political life – serving on juries, holding political office, military service, etc. A history of the Athenian constitution attributed to Aristotle tells us that the Archon Basileus, the one who administered all sacrifices instituted by ancestors and those ritual acts that guaranteed the harmonious functioning of society, was in charge of the torch race, underscoring both the antiquity and religious significance of the event (*Ath. Pol.* 57.1). At the same time, the competitors in the torch race were members of the *ephebeia*, a political institution designed to structure the transition of young Athenian males into political life, and this detail, together with the running of the race according to tribal divisions, emphasizes the many aspects of the torch race that link it to key Athenian political institutions.

Running the torch race as a tribal competition would have provided the city of Athens with a significant occasion for maintaining the group identity of the tribe, and this looks to be the scene portrayed on a bell krater by the Nikias painter, signed by the potter with his father's name and deme. The krater shows two young torch racers on either side of the central scene; in the centre, Nike, the personification of victory, crowns the tribal hero, identified as Antiochus, beside an altar behind which stands an old man wearing a wreath, probably Prometheus. The image suggests that the tribe of Antiochus, to which Nikias' deme also belonged, was victorious in the torch race at the Prometheia, and the bell krater was painted to celebrate the event. Torch races at the Panathenaea and the Prometheia were the subject of the decorations on other vases as well.

Torch races were common to the cult activity of the three gods associated with fire and its technology: Prometheus, Hephaestus, and Athena. Each god had a shrine in the Academy from which the torch race proceeded through the Kerameikos into the city itself. Taking their start from the altar of Prometheus at the Academy, torch races as part of the celebration of Hephaestus and Athena, and others as well, trace a direct link between Prometheus and other major figures of Athenian religious and civic life as well as between the Academy and other significant sites in Athens' topography. A key part of the annual celebrations of these gods, the torch race celebrated fire and its role in making Athens a prosperous and civilized city.

PROMETHEUS, SATYRS, AND FIRE

Both visual and literary evidence bring Prometheus, especially in connection with the torch race, together with satyrs – those hybrid creatures who appear on vases and on the Athenian stage most often in the company of Dionysus and his maenads or nymphs. Satyrs combine the upper body of humans with the hindquarters of a horse, with hooves replacing feet, a horse's tail grafted onto their hindquarters, and pointy ears at the top of their heads. Usually portrayed in a state of permanent erection, their oversized genitalia are more like that of a donkey than a man. At times the sheer animality of the satyr prevails, and yet their extremely grotesque and subversive behaviour is often pointedly related to key aspects of human culture – eating, drinking, sexuality – and they appear in the context of cults, games, and other religious practices. The satyr operates at the boundaries of the human and animal worlds, drawing upon exaggerated humour to critique those very institutions and rituals that define the human sphere. In this respect, satyrs share many aspects of the trickster – 'the grossly erotic, insatiably hungry prankster' – that we discussed in the previous chapter, and it makes perfect sense that the Athenians would bring them into Prometheus' myth, perhaps, as we shall see, as the first recipients of his gift of fire. François Lissarrague has shown that the hybrid world of the satyrs, located on the boundaries between what is animal and what is human, provides a mechanism of cultural scrutiny, especially vis à vis questions of human culture. As a kind of local Athenian trickster figure, the satyr – both in the visual arts and on stage – offers a unique and useful perspective on the significance of Prometheus' gift of fire to the Athenians.

Vase paintings

Representations of Prometheus, holding a fennel stalk in his hand, surrounded by satyrs with torches, were a popular scene on a series of Attic red-figure vases dating from the second half of the fifth century. An Attic calyx-krater (c. 425–420 BC) by the Dinos painter, for example, puts Prometheus and the satyrs together with two other particularly Athenian scenes: the deeds of Theseus and Eos' pursuit of Cephalus, confirming our sense that Prometheus and his gift of fire to mortals have particular significance for Athenians in the fifth century (Fig. 4). On the Dinos krater, the Prometheus scene includes four male figures, one of them a bearded man, standing, with long hair and wearing a belted garment that falls to mid-calf. Five letters identify the bearded man as Prometheus. In both hands he holds a long staff with a flame emerging from a cup-like head. Surrounding this figure are three satyrs, named as Sikinnis, Komos, and Simos. They are dancing and holding lit torches, made from pine shoots that have been tied together. The staff that Prometheus holds is a bit different and has been identified by J. D. Beazley as the narthex, the hollow fennel stalk in which Hesiod and others tell us that Prometheus carried fire down

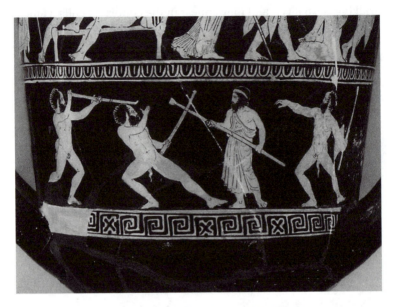

Figure 4 Prometheus and the satyrs (lower band) 1937.983. Dinos painter, Attic calyx-krater, c.425–420 BC

Source: Photo courtesy of Ashmolean Museum, Oxford

to mortals from Zeus. The satyrs, then, are holding the first torches lit by Prometheus' fire and celebrating his gift.

A red-figure bell krater in the museum at Yale University (c. 410 BC) shows a similar scene of Prometheus surrounded by torch-wielding satyrs (Fig. 5). This time, however, the Prometheus figure holds two different kinds of staffs – the narthex in one hand and a torch in the other. Scholars have suggested that this variation represents the moment when Prometheus first gave fire to mankind, perhaps in preparation for the torch race. As Purphoros (Fire-bearer), Prometheus brought fire to mankind, as Purkaeus (Fire-kindler), he lit his first torch, and from that point on, the iconography suggests, men light torches from his altar for races in his honour as well as in honour of other gods. Through these scenes on vases, Athenians invoked the

Figure 5 Prometheus and satyrs 1913. 129. Red-figure bell krater, c. 430–400 BC.

Source: Yale University Art Gallery. Gift of Rebecca Darlington Stoddard

cultural significance of the satyr to link Prometheus' theft of fire from Zeus to the institution of the torch race in Athens. On the stage as well, satyrs and fire provided the city of Athens with a context for celebrating the gifts of Prometheus.

Satyr drama

When the Athenian tragedians produced their tragedies as part of the Dionysiac festivals of the fifth century, they included what is known as a satyr play, and the meddlesome satyric world is a good one for the story of Prometheus. Indeed, the myth of Prometheus' theft of fire – his rebellion against Zeus, king of gods and men, his contest in cleverness, and his actions to save mankind – fits perfectly with what we know about the basic themes and elements of the satyr play. Judging by their titles (*Cyclops*, *Busiris*, *Sciron*, etc.), the topic of many satyr plays included the defeat of a villain or monster, often at the hands of a trickster figure. In addition, like Prometheus' myth and cult, many satyr plays include the theme of bondage and escape as well as the formation of athletic contests and competitions. Satyr plays present stories taken from the mythic world, transformed and subverted through what François Lissarrague has called the 'fun-house mirror' of the satyr world. The erotically supercharged, half-human half-equine satyrs appear on stage as blatant meddlers and creators of disorder, and their dramatic function is to subvert the cohesiveness of the tragic world.

We have evidence that Aeschylus composed a satyr play called *Prometheus Fire-Kindler* that was performed together with the trilogy of which the *Persians* was a part in 472 BC. While the play is not extant, the title suggests that it may have dealt with Prometheus' triumph over and escape from the punishment of Zeus, culminating in the establishment of the torch race as part of the festival in honour of Prometheus. Although it is tempting to argue that the scenes on the vase paintings we just discussed illustrate Aeschylus' Promethean satyr play, their late fifth-century dates make that problematic. Some scholars have suggested that Aeschylus' satyr play was revived on the Athenian stage thirty years after his death, but it is more likely that an association between Prometheus and satyrs remained popular after Aeschylus' death and that later playwrights continued to experiment with the satyric possibilities of Prometheus and his gift of fire.

Aside from the title, only one line can definitely be assigned to the *Prometheus Fire-Kindler*, one that describes how to make long-lasting torches from linen and wax: 'and flax, and pitch and long bands of raw flax' (*TrGF* Fr. 205). Plutarch preserves another passage, however, that may also come from this play, exploiting the humorous potential of the satyrs' first experience with the dangers of fire. He mentions a satyr, who at his first sight of fire, tries to kiss it, but Prometheus warns him not to, saying 'you goat, you will grieve for your (vanished) beard' (*TrGF* Fr. 207). Yet another passage, preserved in a papyrus fragment, may describe the first uses that the satyrs made of fire – chasing nymphs: 'if some Naiad calls me, she will be chased round the firelight. I put my trust in the nymphs who perform dances in honor of Prometheus' gift' (*TrGF* Fr. 204b). The lines that follow, only partially preserved, celebrate Prometheus as the bringer of life (*pheresbios*) and as one who hastens with gifts (*speusidoros*), suggesting a celebration of Prometheus by satyrs and nymphs after his gift of fire to the mortal world.

We might say that Prometheus, together with his torch of fire, hands the Hesiodic role of trickster over to the Athenian satyrs, who continue to elaborate his role in defining and exploring the human condition in a specifically Athenian context. Now it is time to think further about what the cult of Prometheus can tell us about fifth-century Athens. What aspects of the human condition are particularly under scrutiny? What sort of cultural introspection does Prometheus' torch spark among Athenians of this time?

PROMETHEUS, FIRE, AND FIFTH-CENTURY ATHENS

The cult of Prometheus in Athens was primarily a celebration of fire, a tribute to its civilizing potential as well as its destructive power. We have already discussed the ways in which fire was important to Greek religion in general – its significant role in sacrifice, as symbol of divine presence, as medium for communication between gods and men, etc. But now, let us try to narrow that understanding somewhat to ask what Prometheus meant to Athenians in the fifth century BC. By the first quarter of the fifth century, Athenians had first-hand experience of both the best and the worst that fire and its attendant technology could bring to their city. Prometheus was particularly 'good to think with' for fifth-century Athenians living with the immediate aftermath of the Persian invasion.

In the years leading up to the first Persian War, Athens was a prosperous and ambitious city. Starting with the building programme of Peisistratus and his sons in the second half of the sixth century, Athens boasted several buildings and public works of masterful skill. The younger Peisistratus is said to have built an Altar to the Twelve Gods in the Agora in 522, and across the Agora was a small fountain house which brought water in its well-crafted terracotta pipes from a great distance to hundreds of people now frequenting the market-place. Perhaps an even more famous example of water technology was the nine-spouted fountain house built near the bed of the Ilissus river. Southeast of the Acropolis, a monumental temple to Olympian Zeus was begun (although never finished), designed to rival the enormous temples built at that time in Ephesus, Miletus, and on the island of Samos. At the beginning of the fifth century work on a new temple to Athena began on the Acropolis, this one made of Pentelic marble, and of course Pheidias' colossal bronze statue of Athena – so large that her spear and the crest of her helmet could be seen by those sailing to Athens from Sounion – was added to the Acropolis, standing just inside the gateway. Athens was becoming a prosperous and technologically advanced city – living proof of all that Prometheus could bring to a city.

And yet, Athens in all her cultural glory was completely destroyed by the Persians in 480/479. Herodotus tells us that after their victory at Thermopylae, the Persians, led by Xerxes, broke into southern Greece prompting the Athenians to abandon their city. The Persians occupied the citadel, and when Mardonius, Xerxes' general, finally withdrew from Athens in the summer of 479, he left behind a city in ruins. As Herodotus records it, ' he burned Athens, and whatever walls or houses or temples were still upright, he destroyed and demolished' (9.13). Thucydides recalls that 'Of the perimeter wall only small portions were still standing, and most of the houses had fallen, only a few remained in which the Persians leaders had themselves taken quarters' (1.89.3). Archaeological evidence confirms these reports. The Acropolis was looted and burned – the unfinished marble predecessor of the Parthenon as well as the early temple of Athena destroyed. Dozens of statues now in the Acropolis Museum bear witness to the

Persian destruction, while fragments of high-quality pottery show clear effects of the devastating fire. The lower city also burned. Houses, the fortification walls, and sanctuaries, including the Altar of the Twelve Gods, a sanctuary of Zeus and a small temple of Apollo on the west side of the Agora, all were demolished. In short, the city was totally devastated.

Seven years later Aeschylus won first prize at the Dionysiac festival with a dramatic tetralogy that included a tragedy devoted to the defeat of the Persians at Salamis and a satyr play called *Prometheus Fire-Kindler*. We might speculate about the effect of a satyr play devoted to Prometheus' theft of fire and the institution of his cult in Athens performed together with the *Persians*, a tragedy that deals with the defeat of those same people who had invaded Greece and destroyed many temples and shrines within the city of Athens. Aeschylus' *Persians* is the only extant Greek tragedy to deal with a recent historical, rather than mythical, event, and its focus on the suffering and devastation of the Persians must have called to mind the comparable losses of Athenians at an earlier stage of the same war. Part of the power of the play stems precisely from the way that Aeschylus captures a sense of shared suffering in times of war that transcends the individual experience of winners and losers. Certainly the Persian Wars had a strong influence on Aeschylus; he himself fought at the battle of Marathon and lost his brother there. Watching the plays at the Dionysiac festival, then, the Athenian audience may have had a similar ritual experience. The citizens first watched a tragedy devoted to the destruction of the Persians in war – a kind of mirror image of their own wartime losses a decade earlier. Then, looking through the distorted lens of the satyr drama, *Prometheus Fire-Kindler*, the Athenian audience watched Prometheus light the first torch and hand it to the satyrs – hybrid, trickster figures who could help them imagine both the city's need for purification after the devastation of war and its renewed ability to make the best possible use of Prometheus' gift to mankind.

OVERVIEW

Prometheus is linked to Athens through myth and cult; he appears on vase paintings and on the Athenian satyr stage, bringing his gift of fire to the Athenian people. In part, Prometheus' famed intelligence and skill in craft make him a perfect fit for the city of Athena, herself born from Metis, the personification of the clever intelligence for which Prometheus was also famous, and his myth was linked to hers in significant ways. Together with Hephaestus, Prometheus was worshipped in Athens specifically for his association with fire and its attendant technology. His cult was celebrated with torch races that started at his altar in the Academy and traced a route into the city itself, symbolizing perhaps the ritual significance of fire and its prominent role in the civilized life of Athenians.

The Panhellenic myth of Prometheus and his gift of fire took on a more localized and specific meaning, however, within the recent memory of post-Persian War Athens. More than a general celebration of the ambiguous nature of fire or an acknowledgement of its role as a means of communication between gods and men, Prometheus' story offered the Athenians a productive way to think about their own recent trauma. In particular, by putting Prometheus and his initial gift of fire to mankind on the satyr stage, Aeschylus gives the Athenians a chance to start over – to transform their recent memories of fire's destructive capabilities into a city rebuilt and renewed through all the possibilities of technology and the creative intelligence that Prometheus and Athens share. Indeed, Aeschylus was not finished 'thinking with Prometheus', and in the next chapter we will look further at the ways in which he adapted the story of Prometheus to celebrate the progress that mankind made away from the primitive state of the beasts, and in particular the way in which Athens had been able to recreate its city from the ashes and destruction of the Persian Wars into a great city of arts and culture.

3

POLITICAL REBEL AND CULTURAL HERO

Prometheus in Athenian literature

In the previous chapter, we explored the cult of Prometheus in Athens, suggesting that the mythic figure of Prometheus helped fifth-century Athenians think about fire – its beneficial and its destructive potential. In this chapter, we will focus on three literary texts from the classical period. Aeschylus' tragedy *Prometheus Bound* and Plato's philosophical dialogue *Protagoras* show how Prometheus operates in the fifth and fourth centuries as a revolutionary figure on both the political and intellectual stages. Aeschylus' tragic drama *Prometheus Bound* looks to Prometheus, the god who gave fire and hope to mankind, to celebrate the prosperity and power of fifth-century Athens. No longer a trickster figure, Aeschylus' Prometheus adopts the role of a rebel fighting for mankind against the tyranny of Zeus, and his story highlights progress rather than decline as the master narrative of the human condition. Plato's Socratic dialogue *Protagoras* looks to the myth of Prometheus to tell a similar story about man's evolution from an earlier, more bestial state. In Plato's version, however, Prometheus' story highlights social and political skills, rather than technological expertise, as the hallmark of the human condition. In conclusion, we will turn to Aristophanes' comedy *The Birds* to find a comic Prometheus reprising both his trickster and rebel roles in a more humorous vein. The Aristophanic Prometheus, hiding from Zeus under a parasol, is nevertheless a familiar figure, and the comic success of his role as rebel against Zeus and defender of mankind helps confirm our reading of his myth in other Greek sources.

Between Hesiod and the fifth century, poets are curiously silent on the myth of Prometheus, and it is not until the mid-fifth century and Aeschylus' *Prometheus Bound* that we find another extended, literary treatment of the god who stole fire for mankind. Aeschylus is clearly working with Hesiod's Prometheus, and yet the prosperous political and economic context of fifth-century Athens elicits very different aspects of Prometheus' mythic profile. In particular, it was Aeschylus' portrayal of Prometheus as a political rebel that struck a chord with the Romantic poets, who found in his play a powerful mythic background against which to set their own celebration of revolution and rebellion. And so, in addition to discussing the figure of Prometheus in classical Athens, this chapter will serve as a bridge between our discussion of Prometheus in the ancient world and the following discussion of Prometheus at the end of the eighteenth and early nineteenth centuries. Whereas Hesiod's poems claim that all mortal trouble stems from Prometheus' gift of fire, Aeschylus and Plato praise Prometheus as a generous benefactor of mankind, and it would seem that these later authors have in fact turned the Prometheus myth on its head. A closer look, however, will show that it is not the myth that has changed, but rather the material conditions of the human experience that the myth represents.

AESCHYLUS' *PROMETHEUS BOUND*

Of the seventy to ninety titles that are attributed to the Athenian playwright Aeschylus, complete manuscripts of only seven plays have survived. Some scholars have raised the possibility, in part on stylistic grounds and in part on thematic grounds, that the *Prometheus Bound* was not written by Aeschylus. While there is no fifth-century evidence identifying Aeschylus as the author of the play, neither are there any ancient sources that raise questions about the authenticity of the play, and in the absence of clear and compelling evidence one way or the other, most scholars now treat the play as part of the Aeschylean corpus. Aeschylus is said to have liked to compose tetralogies (groups of three tragedies and one satyr play) based on a common theme or myth, and his extant plays show a tendency to work with mythic subjects on a grand scale often structured as a cosmic battle between opposing forces.

Aeschylus' life (c. 525/24–456/55 BC) coincides with the important and decisive series of events in Athens that culminated by the middle of the fifth century with the defeat of the Persians, the development of democratic institutions, and the emergence of Athens as an imperial power. He came of age at the time of the revolution of 508/507 BC that generated the political reforms that many mark as the origin of democracy in Athens (Cleisthenic Reforms) and fought in the great battles that ultimately drove the invading Persians out of Greece: the battle of Marathon (490 BC) and the battles of Salamis (480 BC) and Plataea (479 BC) ten years later. The early 460s BC saw the erasure of a Persian presence in the Aegean, and the following decade heralded some important milestones in the development of democracy, especially the reforms of Ephialtes in 461 BC. In other words, Aeschylus flourished as Athens did. He lived his life when Athens was at the height of its powers, having emerged from Sparta's shadows to assume the leadership not just of Greece, but of an extensive overseas empire as well. And he died before Athens fell to the Spartans in the Peloponnesian Wars at the end of the century. It is in this historical and political milieu that we need to situate our reading of Aeschylus' treatment of the Prometheus myth.

Let us turn briefly first to the plot of the *Prometheus Bound* to provide some context for our discussion of the Prometheus that Aeschylus put on the tragic stage. The play opens on a deserted landscape with two of Zeus' agents, Kratos (Might) and Bia (Force), whom we might remember from Hesiod's *Theogony* as the children of Styx 'who have no home except with Zeus' (*Theogony* 385). Here, they personify the force by which Zeus gained power and compel a reluctant Hephaestus to bind Prometheus to a rocky crag at the limits of the known world (1–87). As the play opens Kratos addresses Hephaestus, reminding him that it was his flower, 'the glow of fire that contains all skill (*pantechnou*)' that Prometheus stole and gave to man:

> It is for these transgressions that he must pay a penalty to the gods so that he may
> learn to love the tyranny of Zeus and to leave off his man-loving (*philanthropou*)
> ways.
>
> (8–11)

Although unwilling, Hephaestus yields to the representatives of Zeus' military force, and shackles Prometheus to the Scythian rock. With their exit, Prometheus is left alone on stage and delivers a monologue taking responsibility for his actions and his punishment:

> I hunted down the secret spring of fire that filled the narthex stem, which was
> revealed to mankind as the teacher of all the arts and a great resource. These
> are the mistakes for which I pay this penalty, nailed with chains under the open
> sky.
>
> (109–13)

With Prometheus thus impaled upon the rocks and unable to move, the rest of the drama unfolds through the arrival and departure of a series of characters. First to join Prometheus on stage is the chorus of twelve to fifteen winged daughters of Ocean. They are surprised to come upon Prometheus and eager to learn why he is being punished so severely. Prometheus replies first with an account of the Titanomachy reminiscent of Hesiod's account in the *Theogony*. He claims that Zeus and the Olympians were victorious only because of Prometheus' advice that they rely upon trickery, not force, to subdue the Titans (221–23). Second, Prometheus explains that Zeus intended to destroy the human race, but that he, Prometheus, rescued them. When pushed by the sympathetic yet prying chorus, Prometheus admits that he went even further: he placed in them blind hopes and he gave them fire (250–54).

At this point in the play Ocean himself enters. In Hesiod, he figured as Prometheus' father-in-law; here, he is no relation, but as a fellow god, he commiserates with Prometheus and offers him help, provided he become a little less outspoken. Prometheus rejects his offers, however, showing himself to be defiant and inflexible, and Ocean storms off in frustration. The daughters of Ocean then deliver a choral song lamenting Zeus' actions, 'this tyrant's deeds', and criticizing his

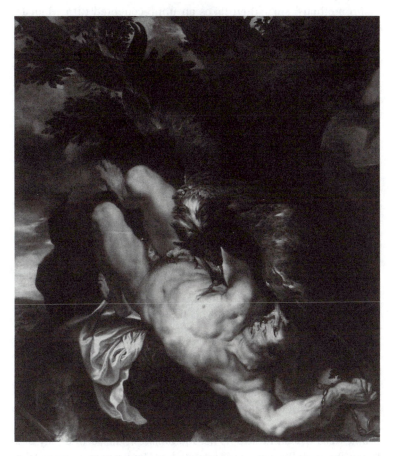

Figure 6 Peter Paul Rubens (1577–1640) and Frans Snyders (1579–1657), *Prometheus Bound*, 1618

Source: Philadelphia Museum of Art. Purchased with the W.P. Wilstach Fund

treatment of fellow gods. Prometheus responds with two speeches outlining all the benefits and practical skills that he has bestowed upon mankind, culminating in the famous boast 'All arts that are mortal come from Prometheus' (506).

Prometheus' story then takes an unprecedented turn when Io appears on stage. Aeschylus was the first to bring Prometheus' myth together with the story of Io, who as Prometheus explains, 'warmed Zeus's heart with love and now she is forced to exercise, running overly long courses, hated by Hera' (590–92). In addition to the dramatic possibilities of pairing an immobile god with a mortal who cannot stand still, the two trace their punishments to a common source. Here, Io tells Prometheus and the chorus how she, too, suffers at the hands of Zeus, doomed to wander across the earth, stung by a gadfly. Prometheus responds by telling her about the son who will be born to her thirteen generations later, Heracles. He is the one who will one day liberate Prometheus from his punishment. Prometheus consoles Io with the promise that soon Zeus himself will suffer, for Zeus will eventually make a marriage that will hurt him – his wife will bear a son stronger than his father. Prometheus alone knows the secret that will save Zeus from his fate.

Finally, Hermes appears, a messenger of Zeus, and demands that Prometheus reveal this secret knowledge in clear and certain terms. When Prometheus refuses to comply, Hermes offers new punishments – an eagle that will daily devour his flesh. Again, Prometheus rejects Hermes and the play ends with a catastrophic conflagration and Prometheus' final defiant words, 'you see me, how I suffer, how unjustly'.

After setting up such a powerful opposition between Zeus and Prometheus, the story feels unresolved – especially to those familiar with the whole myth. Indeed, a scholiast to the play remarks that Prometheus is released in the next play, and many scholars believe this to be the *Prometheus Unbound* (*Prometheus Luomenos*), the second play of a trilogy in which Prometheus is liberated by Heracles from his shackles and the daily visit by the eagle. For in addition to the *Prometheus Bound*, we have fragments of this and a third play, *Prometheus Fire-Bearer* (*Prometheus Purphoros*), attributed to Aeschylus, suggesting that the *Prometheus Bound* was part of a thematically-connected trilogy along the lines of Aeschylus' *Oresteia*. The final play, *Prometheus Fire-Bearer*, is thought to celebrate the reconciliation of Zeus and Prometheus and the inauguration of Prometheus' torch race in Athens as part of the celebration of his gift to mankind.

In the *Prometheus Bound*, Aeschylus closely follows Hesiod's two accounts of Prometheus. As in the *Theogony*, the fifth-century play locates Prometheus' actions on behalf of mankind within the larger cosmic frame of the Titanomachy and Zeus' eventual acquisition of power. Both authors emphasize the intellectual cleverness of Prometheus, and their accounts are concerned primarily with the origin of humans and their relationship with the gods. That said, Aeschylus makes some striking changes to Hesiod's version. Perhaps most conspicuous are the absences: no deceptive sacrifice at Mekone, no Pandora. Prometheus is no longer the son of Iapetos and Klymene but rather of Gaia herself. While his brother Atlas is mentioned as a fellow sufferer, there is no Menoitios and no Epimetheus in Aeschylus' play. These and other more subtle changes combine to portray a very different Prometheus, this one, as we will see, well-suited to the political and cultural experience of fifth-century Athens.

FROM TRICKSTER TO REBEL

While Aeschylus continues to locate Prometheus' gift of fire within the story of Zeus' rise to power, the nature of Zeus' rule is very different, and this change has a profound impact on Prometheus' story. In the *Theogony*, the story of Prometheus' (failed) attempt to deceive Zeus is introduced as part of an elaborate sequence of actions designed to consolidate and celebrate Zeus' power. The poem presents Zeus at the end of the process of his emergence as a ruler. He has successfully combined the use of force with intellectual prowess, and he has further cemented his authority through selective and significant alliances, not the least of which was his marriage to Mnemosyne, mother of the Muses who sing a song of celebration of his rule. In this context, the clever and tricky Prometheus is introduced to engage Zeus in a context of wits, and Zeus' triumph over Prometheus in the end is the ultimate expression of his own native intelligence. Furthermore, within this context, Prometheus functions as a trickster figure whose deceptive theft of fire actually brings humans sorrow and work rather than any benefits or advantages.

In the *Prometheus Bound*, however, the context for the conflict between Prometheus and Zeus is very different. Here, Prometheus' actions constitute a rebellion against the cruelty of Zeus' authoritarian regime. Aeschylus' Zeus is new to power, and his rule is raw and cruel. As George Thomson describes him, 'Zeus is a tyrant and his rule is a tyranny', an assessment that is repeated over and over by most of the characters in the play. His ministers are Might and Force; he is suspicious of his friends, impervious to persuasion, and, as we see from his treatment of Io, he is prone to violence (Thomson 1972: 322–23).

Aeschylus has thus changed the very nature of the conflict between Prometheus and Zeus from a contest of wits to a political rebellion. By making Zeus out to be an insecure and power-hungry tyrant, Aeschylus invokes a political designation with specific negative connotations in fifth-century Athens. Although in its early uses the word *tyrannos* merely designated one whose sole rule was not inherited, by the fifth century, tyrants were known to be hubristic rulers with a tendency towards violence and a belief that they were a law unto themselves. Athens, in particular, was famous for its hatred of tyranny, linking the foundation of its democratic traditions to the moment when Harmodius and Aristogeiton, thereafter celebrated as the Tyrannicides, delivered their city from the despotism of the sons of Peisistratus. Zeus of the *Prometheus Bound* embodies the qualities associated with this historical memory of tyranny, and in this political context, Zeus' punishment of Prometheus takes on the perspective of recent history. Carried out by Force and Might, his shackling of Prometheus to a rock replicates the kind of violent disregard for others that typifies tyrannical regimes. Zeus appears rough on mortals as well. Whereas in the *Theogony* he withholds fire from mortals in response to Prometheus' trickery at the sacrifice at Mekone, in the *Prometheus Bound*, Zeus' intention to destroy the mortal race is completely unmotivated. Aeschylus' Prometheus is thus less of a trickster and more of a rebel, an advocate for mankind against the oppression of the gods. As he explains to the chorus, when Zeus threatened to blot out the race of mankind and create a new one, Prometheus alone was willing to stand up for mortals against Zeus' abuse of power. The rebellious aspect of Prometheus' character is something that the

Romantics explore in much more detail, as we will see in the following chapter.

FROM HOPE TO PROPHECY

In addition to recasting Hesiod's trickster figure as a rebel, Aeschylus adapts the myth to enhance Prometheus' prophetic rather than deceptive powers in the play. Prometheus is the son of Gaia, not Klymene, in this play, and Aeschylus tells us that it was Prometheus, not Gaia as in Hesiod's account, who gave Zeus the key advice that enabled him to defeat the Titans. Gaia warned her son that 'not by strength nor overmastering force but by guile only' would victory over the Titans be achieved, and Prometheus passed on this vital information to Zeus, who took advantage of Prometheus' inside knowledge to triumph over the Titans and emerge as the king of the gods. In addition to having access to information that enabled Zeus' triumph over the Titans, Prometheus holds important knowledge about Zeus' impending marriage that would save him from downfall (an aspect also not present in Hesiod's tale) if he should share it with Zeus – and this exclusive knowledge of the future only adds fuel to the fire of the stand-off between the two gods.

Most conspicuously, Prometheus' name is etymologized as 'fore-thought' at the end of Kratos' opening speech:

The Gods named you 'Forethought' falsely, for you yourself need forethought to find a way to escape from this device.

(85–87)

In Hesiod's poems Prometheus is characterized as clever, smart, and insightful, and his ability to think ahead is implied in the *Works and Days* through his advice to his oppositely named brother Epimetheus. Yet, Hesiod neither emphasizes Prometheus' own prophetic powers nor, with the exception of the problematic Hope tucked inside Pandora's jar, does he include strategies for dealing with the future as part of Prometheus' legacy to mankind. Aeschylus, however, makes this a key aspect of his Prometheus myth.

Hope, we remember, remained trapped in Pandora's jar once all the other evils and troubles that came to characterize human existence were released into the world. While Aeschylus omits Pandora from his Prometheus story, he plucks Hope from the jar of evils and gives it a kind of prominence and positive value not present in Hesiod's version. In his opening conversation with the chorus of Oceanids, hope is the first thing that Prometheus mentions as his gift to mankind:

> P: I stopped mortals from foreseeing their fate.
> Ch: What kind of cure did you discover for this sickness?
> P: Blind hopes I placed in them.
> Ch: This is a great benefit you gave to men.
> P: Besides this, I gave them fire.
> Ch: And now do creatures of the day possess bright-faced fire?
> P: Yes, from which they will learn many skills.
>
> (248–54)

Fire and its capacity for teaching all crafts are relegated to second billing here. Prometheus' first benefaction is designed to help mortals cope with the future, although the ambivalence surrounding the nature of hope has not entirely been erased. When the chorus asks Prometheus 'What kind of cure did you discover for this sickness?', the word here for cure, *pharmakon*, is also the word for poison, preserving some of the same ambiguities in assessing the nature of hope present in Hesiod's version. And yet the 'blind hope' of this passage has a more positive sense as we can see by the chorus' response: 'That is a great benefit you gave to men.' While its blindness may hamper mortal knowledge of the future, hope also allows man to ignore his impending death and to live with zest, free to accomplish things he might not otherwise have attempted.

And so, Prometheus' gift of hope, together with that of fire, is given in the spirit of help, as a mortal strategy for coping with imperfect knowledge and control of the future. Prometheus not only gave mortals technology – as we will discuss further – but also hope for the future. This is part of Aeschylus' emphasis on forethought as important to Prometheus' myth – it is the very essence of his name and a key element of his legacy to humankind. Mortals, by definition, will die, and Prometheus could do nothing about that. Instead he replaced foresight of their doom with blind hopes about the future and gave them fire and all the other crafts that enable mortals to prolong life and to improve its quality. Hope is part of the human experience – another thing that separates mankind from the omniscient gods.

PROMETHEUS AND PROGRESS

While the Greeks may not have had a specific word for progress, they certainly did have in Prometheus a good myth for thinking about the inherent ambiguity of the concept. The notion of progress implies a goal or direction in which things get better, but this admittedly vague definition in turn assumes a series of value judgements. How is progress to be measured? By happiness? By mankind's control over nature? By material wealth? The ancient Greeks were no more unanimous on the definition of progress than we are today. Then, as now, however, technology served as an important indicator of progress, and in this respect, Prometheus' mythic role as the bringer of fire to mankind made him a logical choice for meditations on the benefits and risks that stem from technological innovations and advances.

To see how this works, we will return to Aeschylus' *Prometheus Bound*. 'Besides,' Prometheus adds in his speech to the chorus, 'I gave them fire. . . . from which they will learn many skills.' By suppressing the Mekone episode that gave Zeus the motive to withhold fire in Hesiod, Aeschylus creates a very simple and purely benevolent context for Prometheus' gift to mankind of fire – an attempt to thwart Zeus' plan to destroy the mortal race. Before fire, men were no better off than beasts; with fire, Prometheus explains that humans will be able to develop all skills and crafts necessary to create a better world for themselves. The Greek word for craft, *techne*, from which we get our words 'technology' and 'technique', encompasses the arts, skills, and crafts that mark civilized human existence, ranging from metallurgy and agriculture to pottery and poetry. By contrast to Hesiod, who characterized Prometheus' gift of fire as the cause of mankind's fall from the Golden Age to the hard-working Iron Age, Aeschylus'

Prometheus helps articulate one of the earliest and certainly most detailed accounts of progress in Greek literature.

In his first speech, Prometheus explains that before he intervened men lived like animals:

> Listen to the troubles that men had – how I gave them, who had no wits, the use of their intelligence and their minds. I will tell you this not because I blame men, but to explain the benevolence behind my gift. For first, although men had eyes, they could not see; although they had ears, they could not hear; instead, like the shapes of dreams they conducted all matters in confusion for their whole long life. They did not know how to build brick houses facing the sun, nor how to work with wood. But they lived like swarming ants in the sunless hollows of caves. For them there was no sure sign of winter nor of flowering spring nor of fruit-bearing summer. But they did everything without judgment until I showed them the risings of stars and their settings that are hard to detect. And calculation – the best of all skills – I discovered for them and the combination of letters, a source of memory of all things, mother of the muses, a skilled worker. And I was the first to yoke beasts in traces to be subject to the yokes and the saddle so that they might bear the greatest burden for men. And I harnessed horses that love the reins and led them to the carriage, the crown of wealthy luxury. No one else but me discovered linen-winged wagons for sailors. Such are the contrivances I discovered for men, poor me, and yet I have not the cleverness with which to escape my present trouble.

> (442–71)

Prometheus begins by describing a world far from Hesiod's Golden Age, one in which men were little more than beasts before Prometheus intervened and made them 'masters of their minds'. With no tools, no skills, they live at the whim of nature – like ants swarming in the ground. Next, Prometheus launches into a list of discoveries that he made to improve the quality of human life, and in a second speech, he elaborates these contributions even further:

> Listen to the rest and marvel still more at the kinds of skills and resources I devised. This is the greatest – if someone fell sick, formerly there was no cure, neither food, ointment, nor drink, but they wasted away through need of medicine before I showed them the mixing of mild remedies with which they could ward off all

disease. And I arranged many ways of prophecy. I was the first to judge what things from dreams come true in the waking hours; I interpreted for them the cries of birds, hard to determine, and omens seen on the way. And of the flight of birds with bent claws, I carefully explained for them which ones were favorable by nature and the sinister ones – what habitat each had, which ones preyed on each other, and which sat together. Also I explained the smoothness of the entrails, what color the bile should be to please the gods, and the varied beauty of the lobes. I wrapped thigh bones in fat and the long shank bone and burned them, putting mankind on the road to this difficult art. And I opened their eyes to the flaming signs, formerly obscure. So much for these things – beneath the earth, the hidden benefits to mankind: bronze, iron, silver, and gold. Who could say he discovered them before me? No one, I know for sure, who would speak the truth. Here is the whole story in a nutshell – all arts for mortals come from Prometheus.

(476–506)

Prometheus highlights three main arenas in which he has improved the lot of mankind: medicine, prophecy, and metallurgy. It comes as a bit of a surprise that Prometheus makes no mention of his gift of fire here, nor does he focus on those technological skills that depend upon fire. In addition, his invention of sacrifice – so important to the logic of Hesiod's Prometheus story – is embedded within the broader category of prophetic skills or ways to predict the future. In the absence of fire and sacrifice, intellectual developments and skills are emphasized as Prometheus' legacy to mankind. Taking both speeches together, we can make out two different threads of his argument.

First, Prometheus emphasizes the chaotic and undeveloped nature of mankind's prior existence. Before his intervention, men lived like animals. He then proceeds to elaborate this savage beast-like existence negatively – by listing all the skills that they did not have: no carpentry to build houses, no astronomy to predict weather or maximize the harvest of crops, no strategies for coping with sickness: 'all their doings were indeed without judgment'.

Second, Prometheus offers a list of the inventions and skills that he bestowed upon mankind, explaining that it was he who set mankind on the road to civilization. In addition to astronomy, he discovered for them counting, writing, animal husbandry, ships, medicine, prophecy, sacrifice, and metallurgy. In short, Aeschylus' Prometheus tells a story of progress. His myth represents the human condition in terms of hope and improvement, as an evolution away from a primitive state of nature towards a more civilized human existence.

Aeschylus celebrates Prometheus as responsible for all of Athens' cultural strengths: together with his gift of fire, Prometheus gives mankind the tools to conquer the future, to make it a better place. His gift of fire stands as a symbol of all the skill and knowledge that combine to distinguish human existence from that of animals. Instead of focussing on the break with the gods, as Hesiod does, Aeschylus devotes his attention to the other end of the god/human/animal spectrum – to the ways in which the human experience surpasses that of beasts. In composing this speech for Prometheus, Aeschylus no doubt drew upon contemporary theories of progress as well as other traditional modes of describing human development. By the middle of the fifth century, rationalizing views of man's development began to be taught by natural philosophers such as Anaximander, Democritus, and Protagoras. Protagoras and others were part of a group of intellectuals known as the Sophists who travelled throughout Greece offering a new kind of education that, among other things, challenged some of the familiar and traditional social and political institutions. And if we turn now to Plato's *Protagoras*, a philosophical dialogue in which the great thinker himself appears, we find yet again the myth of Prometheus linked to a tale of progress.

PLATO'S PROTAGORAS

While Plato's *Protagoras* was probably written in the 390s BC, it is set in Athens in the late 430s BC, and so it makes sense to discuss it now before moving ahead to the end of the fifth century to look at Aristophanes' *Birds*. In the dialogue, Protagoras, Socrates, and the others are engaged in a discussion about the nature of civic virtue (*arete*) – is it innate in humans or are men taught the skill by others? After the preliminary scenes of the dialogue, the sophist Protagoras uses the myth of Prometheus to argue that while virtue can be acquired and cultivated from others, nevertheless all mortals have a share of it.

To this end, Plato's *Protagoras* tells a story of man's evolutionary development from a 'naked state, without shoes, bed, or weapons' thanks to Prometheus' gift of 'wisdom in the arts together with fire'.

Prometheus appears elsewhere in the Platonic dialogues. In the *Gorgias* (523d–e), Socrates has Prometheus prevent men's fore-knowledge of their death. In the *Philebus* (16c), Socrates explains that through 'some Prometheus' the gods gave humans not just fire, but also the way in which 'all the inventions of art [*techne*] have been brought to light'. But it is in the *Protagoras* that Plato introduces the myth of Prometheus at great length. While the *Protagoras* brings together a host of prominent Athenian intellectual figures to discuss the Sophists and their claims to teach wisdom and virtue, it is the conversation between Socrates and Protagoras that forms the heart of the dialogue. When Protagoras claims to make men good citizens, Socrates asks the great Sophist to demonstrate whether, in fact, civic virtue is teachable or not. After all, he explains, not even the great Pericles was able to impart his own civic expertise to his sons. In agreeing to do so, Protagoras chooses the pleasing form of a fable (*muthos*) as the format for his presentation.

At the beginning of the world, Protagoras explains, the gods moulded the forms of living creatures out of a mixture of earth and fire, and then when they were about to bring these beings into the light, they charged Prometheus and his brother Epimetheus with the duty of endowing them with the necessary qualities and skills to survive. Epimetheus begged his brother to let him apportion these things to all creatures, and Prometheus agreed to oversee his brother's work once it was done. Epimetheus began distributing powers to the various beasts taking care that no one species be extinguished. When Prometheus arrived on the scene, however, he found that his brother had bungled the job:

> Now Epimetheus, being not so very wise, did not notice that he had squandered his stock of properties on the animals while the race of men was left unequipped, and he did not know what to do. As he was thinking about it, Prometheus arrived to examine his distribution, and he saw that the other creatures were fully and suitably provided for but that man was naked, without shoes, bed, or weapons.

> (321b–c)

Much dismayed and pressured by the arrival of the day on which man was due to emerge from the earth, Prometheus took steps to ensure the survival of mankind:

> Then Prometheus, unsure about what kind of protection he could discover for man, stole from Hephaestus and Athena skill in the arts together with fire – since without fire this skill could not be acquired or used – and gave it to man.
>
> (321 c–d).

Now, Protagoras explains, man had acquired the wisdom of daily life, but he still lacked civic wisdom, for that remained in the possession of Zeus.

Protagoras proceeds to elaborate the improved state of the human experience in light of Prometheus' gift. He explains that since man had a portion of the divine, he alone worshipped gods and built altars and holy images for them. In addition, mankind soon acquired the skills of speech and words, and discovered dwellings, clothes, sandals, beds, and the goods that are of the earth (322a). But, Protagoras continues, in spite of these skills, men were not able to live together peacefully in groups and soon began to perish. At this point in Protagoras' myth, Zeus intervenes to save mankind. He sends Hermes down to give shame and justice to mankind – not just to some but to all since cities cannot be formed if only a few have a share of these arts. Hence, Protagoras explains that civic virtue is the business of all – it is the very essence of being human:

> For they say that everyone should say that they are just, whether they are or not, and whoever does not make some claim to justice is mad; since it is necessary that everyone have a portion of it in some way unless he is not of human kind.
>
> (323b–c)

Protagoras then concludes his telling of the Prometheus myth by explaining that this is why though some have specific skills, all have a share in the civic arts. He maintains that this virtue is teachable and proceeds to prove this to Socrates by means of argument, not myth, in the next section of the dialogue.

The historian of ancient philosophy W.K.C. Guthrie points out that

> what Protagoras seems to have done in this story is to construct, partly at least from existing fifth-century Ionian philosophy, a rationalistic account of the origin of animal and human life, and of human civilization, and graft on to it the tale of Prometheus and Epimetheus, which not unnaturally has undergone some modification in the process.

(Guthrie 1957: 88)

Indeed, here, as in Aeschylus' play, Plato's *Protagoras* links Prometheus with the development of the intellectual and cultural skills that separate humans from the beasts. And yet, although he invokes a familiar mythic figure and plot, Plato's *Protagoras* alters the traditional version in three important ways.

First, it looks as though Protagoras has reversed the traditional roles of Prometheus and Epimetheus in the Prometheus myth. Whereas Hesiod has each brother fulfil the etymological potential of his name, in Plato's version it is Epimetheus who acts first, and Prometheus who takes action after the fact. Upon closer inspection, however, we see that switching their roles does not actually take either brother out of character – it is only that they have switched positions in the narrative. Epimetheus remains 'not so very smart after all' and Prometheus is still the one to have the foresight to provide for mankind in some way. By reversing the order, but not the nature, of their actions in the myth, Protagoras' Prometheus tells a very different story from that of Hesiod – one of survival and intelligence rather than punishment and decline. In addition, this kind of role reversal removes the stark comparison between the two brothers. In its place, Protagoras' retelling fleshes out each brother with respect to the other, arguing for a richer combination of both forethought and reflection. Prometheus should have known not to entrust his brother with such an important responsibility while Epimetheus' actions on behalf of the other animals are not entirely without intelligence. In Protagoras' version, then, Epimetheus is no mere foil for his more thoughtful brother, but rather embodies a similar mixture of forethought and afterthought as does Prometheus himself.

This reconfiguration of the Prometheus/Epimetheus dynamic has interesting implications for what the dialogue has to say about institutions of the production and dissemination of knowledge. Plato returns to the Prometheus myth at the end of the *Protagoras* when Socrates observes that he and Protagoras have reversed their initial positions. In suggesting that they work their way back through their discussion to see where they went astray, Socrates invokes the two brothers:

> And I would like to work our way through these things until we get at what virtue is and then reconsider whether it is teachable or not, lest that Epimetheus deceive us in our investigation just as he overlooked us in his distribution, as you said. I like the Prometheus of your fable better than the Epimetheus; for making use of him, I take forethought [*promethoumenos*] for my own life as I work on all these questions.
>
> (361c–d)

Plato's introduction of Prometheus extends beyond the internal discussion of whether virtue is teachable or not to the very framework of a philosophical investigation of the nature of knowledge and wisdom.

Second and even more interesting, Plato has completely transformed the role of Zeus in the myth. Instead of being hostile to Prometheus and humans, he acts together with Prometheus as co-benefactor of mankind. Plato omits the sacrifice component of Prometheus' myth as reason for their enmity. Indeed, we might even wonder why Prometheus had to steal the fire at all. By downplaying the hostility between Prometheus and Zeus, Plato completely defuses the political tension of Aeschylus' version. Neither Hesiod's trickster figure nor Aeschylus' political rebel, Plato's Prometheus emerges as a symbol of the importance of political skills and civic virtue in the human sphere. The Protagorean Prometheus story focuses less on technology and other ways in which mankind has learned to master nature, and instead highlights mankind's need and ability to form social groups as a distinctive human quality. Humans are different from animals by virtue of their need to live together in communities – both for practical reasons of self-defence and in order to benefit from social contacts and communication.

By highlighting justice or civic virtue as Prometheus' legacy to mankind, Plato again overturns a major theme of Hesiod's version.

Whereas in the *Works and Days*, justice is one of the many Golden Age ideals that were lost to mankind as a result of Prometheus' theft of fire, here, it is justice that emerges from the joint actions of Prometheus and Zeus. Plato's Protagoras turns to Prometheus to argue that it is justice, or civic virtue, that defines the human condition. He concludes the mythic narrative by claiming that everyone partakes of justice to some extent – not to do so would exclude one from the human race.

Finally, while Plato's Prometheus myth erases all traces of Aeschylus' political conflict, it does articulate an intellectual revolution of sorts. It has been argued that Protagoras' retelling of the Prometheus myth is a 'promethean' or subversive act in itself. After all, the aims of the Sophistic education with which Protagoras was associated were at heart revolutionary. They rejected the traditional models of education and the established structures of political and social power associated with Olympian religion in favour of more rationalistic modes of thought and reason – the kind of clever thinking associated with Prometheus. By downplaying the traditional, political hostility between Zeus and Prometheus, Protagoras' Prometheus thus joins the Sophist's own work to the very traditions and conventions that the larger Sophistic movement was replacing. When Protagoras claims that his teachings create good citizens, men who will be powerful and influential within the city-state, he is, in fact, advocating a kind of training that undermines the conventional modes of power in Athens. By setting up Zeus together with Prometheus as those who bestow civic virtue upon mankind, Protagoras acknowledges the conventional authority of Zeus all the while that he challenges its power with the resourceful Promethean aspects of his teaching.

While Aeschylus structures Prometheus' gift of fire to mankind as a political act, a noble revolt against the privilege of tyrannic power, Plato highlights Prometheus' role in subverting and transforming the nature of civic participation that separates men from the beasts. Both, however, celebrate the uniquely human qualities of foresight, planning, strategy, and intelligence – characteristics that separate humans from animals and take us closer to the world of the divine. In particular, Aeschylus and Plato both combine contemporary rational discourse about the progress of mankind with a traditional mythic narrative – the story of Prometheus' theft of fire. What emerges is the extent to which Prometheus operates as a revolutionary figure in intellectual as well as political terms.

THE COMIC PROMETHEUS

Aristophanes, the comic poet, was one of the last major fifth-century Athenian authors to invoke the myth of Prometheus. In the *Birds*, a comedy written and performed in 414 BC, Prometheus appears toward the end of the play (1494–1552) to advise the play's protagonist, Pisthetairos. At the play's beginning, Pisthetairos and his sidekick, Euelpides have fled an overly litigious and contentious Athens in search of a better life. They join forces with the birds and attempt to set up a utopia in the sky, Cloudcuckooland. When the gods grow angry at the situation – the new city has cut off all sacrifices from earth to Olympus – Prometheus arrives to help negotiate a peace treaty of sorts between the new city and the gods. He tells Pisthetairos that a divine delegation is on the way to the city but that the birds must only make peace if 1) Zeus restores his sceptre to them and 2) he surrenders the girl Basileia to Pisthetairos in marriage. Prometheus leaves the stage shortly thereafter, and the action of the play proceeds precisely along the lines of this advice.

In terms of the plot, Prometheus' role in the *Birds* recalls both Hesiod and Aeschylus' versions of his myth. As in Hesiod, where Prometheus intervened in the Titanomachy to help the rebel children of Kronos led by Zeus in their fight with the other Titans, here, too, Prometheus helps the birds in their war with the gods. In each case, Prometheus functions as an adviser of sorts; he has important information about how the enemy can be beaten. While in Aeschylus' *Prometheus Bound*, Prometheus helps Zeus in his battle against the older generation, here in the *Birds*, he helps Pisthetairos and the birds against Zeus. The obvious reason for his change of sides is the horrific treatment that he has received at the hands of an ungrateful Zeus in Aeschylus' drama – a play which the *Birds* appears to echo in several places. In the *Birds*, it is clear that Prometheus has been released from his sufferings and restored to the community of gods so that he can report on their current food shortages.

Sacrifice continues to play a key role in Prometheus' story as well – here it is the interruption of the communicative flow of sacrificial offerings from humans to the gods that motivates Prometheus' intervention in the play. Heracles, too, remains part of Prometheus' story. In both Hesiod and Aeschylus, we remember, Heracles occupies an important position at the end of the myth – he is the one who, thirty thousand years later, kills the liver-devouring eagle and releases Prometheus from his punishment. In the *Birds*, he appears together with Poseidon and Tryballos to broker the actual peace between the birds and men (in part so that he can get at the barbeque) that concludes the play. While Prometheus comes to Pisthetairos with the plan for getting what they want from the gods, he remains a problematic trickster figure in the play – he must remain under cover and cannot actually get the deal done. Heracles, on the other hand, is the one who is able to negotiate the peace. Heracles, himself part human and part divine and full of bestial appetites, is another mythic figure who, like Prometheus, negotiates the boundaries between gods, men, and beasts. While the myth of Prometheus as trickster and rebel helps articulate the break or the gap between gods and men, Heracles' story offers a model for a more successful negotiation of those boundaries, and it is for this reason perhaps that he is so closely connected to the resolution of Prometheus' story.

The Aristophanic Prometheus continues to function as a friend of mankind and foe of the gods, following very much in the tradition of Hesiod and Aeschylus, but with a comic twist – his proverbial cleverness here transformed into a kind of nervous caution. As he comes on stage with his garment covering his head and carrying a parasol, he keeps a series of protective layers between himself and the watchful eye of Zeus: 'Oh me, oh my. I hope that Zeus doesn't see me!' (1494) A few lines later he implores Pisthetairos not to mention his name: 'You'll ruin me, if Zeus sees me here. But so that I can tell you all the news from up above, take this parasol of mine and hold it up so that the gods won't see me' (1506–1509) To which Pisthetairos replies admiringly: 'Oooh – you're really thinking now – and with forethought!' (1510–11) with a pun on Prometheus' name that recalls Aeschylus' use of the same wordplay in the *Prometheus Bound*.

While neither the dignified rebel of Aeschylus' drama nor the devious trickster of Hesiod's poems, the Aristophanic Prometheus retains elements of both, thereby confirming their significance for interpretations of Prometheus. He is part clever rogue, bringing important information to humans, and part rebel; above all, he is the master of information, still moving between the world of gods and men – even while skulking beneath his umbrella. While Prometheus is but a bit player in Aristophanes' *Birds*, the comic success of his role in the play hinges upon the entire array of mythic resonances that he brings with him – trickster, rebel, thief of fire, master of information, and friend of mankind, especially in Athens.

OVERVIEW

In conclusion, we are struck again by the incredible elasticity of the Prometheus myth. Aeschylus and Plato have completely inverted the story of decline and fall told by Hesiod's Prometheus while Aristophanes plays with both of these traditions to comic effect. The key elements are still there – Prometheus steals fire for mankind and is punished for it – and yet the story that the myth tells is very different. While Hesiod's version laments mankind's fall from the Golden Age and their proximity to the gods, the Prometheus of Aeschylus and Plato celebrates the progress that mankind has made away from a state of nature, side by side with the beasts. It all depends on where you start, and yet in spite of their different conclusions, each of these authors turns to Prometheus to grapple with the human condition, staking out a place for mankind somewhere between gods and beasts. Moreover, each elaborates the nature of the human condition in terms of those institutions and practices that separate mankind from beasts and gods, particularly agriculture and sacrifice. Hesiod's *Works and Days* emphasizes the necessity and difficulty of work for mankind. Aeschylus' *Prometheus Bound*, on the other hand, celebrates those technological accomplishments that Prometheus' gift has enabled mankind to make – building houses, sailing the seas, etc. – and calls them progress. Plato's *Protagoras* highlights the civic skills that allow mankind to live together in political communities, to move beyond mere survival towards a truly more civilized human experience. Through times of scarce resources and those of great wealth and power, on both the tragic and the comic stage, in myth and cult, the figure of Prometheus helps fifth-century Athenians think about what it means to be human. And it will continue to do so in a variety of historical and cultural contexts, as we will see from our discussion of the Prometheus myth in the nineteenth and twentieth centuries.

PROMETHEUS AFTERWARDS

4

THE ROMANTIC PROMETHEUS

In the previous three chapters we have seen the ways in which the Greeks celebrated Prometheus as fire thief, political rebel, and symbol of human progress and potential. Hesiod's Prometheus is a trickster figure responsible for the bleak nature of the human experience in archaic Greece while in the fifth-century BC, Prometheus' myth offers Athenian poets and philosophers a productive framework for thinking more positively about revolution (both political and intellectual) and mankind's progress towards a more civilized and prosperous existence. Turning now to the Romantic period, it is Prometheus' dual role as defiant rebel and creator of humans that captures the imagination of European poets and writers. While Prometheus did not completely fall out of favour in the intervening years – in the early Christian tradition Prometheus was fused with Christ as twin symbols of human suffering, and he was certainly an important source for Milton's figure of Satan in *Paradise Lost* – the combined force of his political potential and his creative spirit made Prometheus particularly well-suited to those poets and writers who, having experienced the promises and the disappointments of the French Revolution, were looking for new models of heroism on the political and artistic stage.

Originating in Germany and England during the 1790s, the Romantic movement, with its focus on creativity, imagination, and freedom, spread, albeit with considerable modifications, throughout Europe between 1800 and 1830. Rather than offer a general overview of Prometheus' influence on Romanticism, this chapter will focus on a handful of influential writers in the late eighteenth and early nineteenth centuries for whom Prometheus played a key role in their imaginative vision to transform the world. For Goethe, Byron, and the Shelleys, Prometheus was at once the rebel against authority, the symbol of human suffering, and the creator of mankind – it was the richness of Prometheus as a mythic archetype that made all this possible.

GOETHE'S PROMETHEUS AND ARTISTIC CREATIVITY

Johann Wolfgang Goethe's (1749–1832) position on the threshold of European Romanticism, a movement that he did much to shape and influence, offers a good place to begin our study of the Romantic Prometheus. Goethe, the first German writer of unquestioned European stature, made his mark early with the publication of a sentimental novel, *The Sorrows of Young Werther*, at the age of 25 (1774), and continued to enjoy a long and productive career working in a range of literary genres. Goethe enjoyed extraordinary literary success during his life, and his authority and status as 'the genuine and proper embodiment of German art' grew even more in the nineteenth century. In the wake of the unification of Germany in 1871, the universalism and cosmopolitanism of Goethe's works, it was claimed, helped Germans shake off their local patriotisms and find their new identity as a nation-state.

Throughout Goethe's long and productive career the myth of Prometheus appears at regular intervals. In 1773, he composed two acts of a drama called *Prometheus* (which was published in 1830). In the play, Prometheus appears as the defiant son of Zeus who insists on creating a human realm on his own terms and teaches men to cope with the earthly existence that he has given them. In the following year, he composed a lyric ode to Prometheus drawing upon the same themes. The figure of Prometheus certainly infused his lifelong work, *Faust* (1773–1832) – both protagonists are creators, rebels and advocates for mankind who, once loyal servants of God, subsequently turn away from and then finally are reconciled with the divine force. In 1808, in a fragmentary epic on the nature of the human race called *Pandora*, Goethe adapted Prometheus' role as symbol of the eternal conflict between gods and men to dramatize the battling forces within human nature.

In addition to these poetic works, Goethe looked to the mythological potential of Prometheus to reflect upon his own experience as a young man and poet. In 1813–14, in a work called *Poetry and Truth*, Goethe explains that Prometheus represented for him a genius that would mediate between gods and men. As he put it, 'The fable of Prometheus became living in me/ The old titan web I cut up according to my measurements.' Prometheus exerted a powerful influence upon Goethe as artist. Cut off from traditional sources of authority (religious, paternal, political) and alienated from the literary aesthetic and political sympathies of his peers, Goethe found in the rebellious nature and creative power of Prometheus a powerful model for his own artistic and personal autonomy. In particular, it was Prometheus' act of creating mankind, not his theft of fire or rebellion against Zeus, that helped Goethe explore the possibilities and limitations of the creative process. What is the role of the artist in society? What is the nature of the creative process?

Although Prometheus permeates Goethe's work, it is the free-verse hymn to Prometheus (1773) that looks most clearly to Prometheus' myth to celebrate artistic genius and poetry as the ultimate affirmation of identity. The poem scorns the power of Jupiter and eulogizes, in its place, the power of human creativity. The poem opens with an imperative – Prometheus dares Zeus to 'cover your heavens' – and goes on to contrast the Olympian world of Zeus with his own:

> Still you must leave
> My earth intact
> And my small hovel, which you did not build,
> And this my hearth
> whose glowing heat
> You envy me.

(6–11)

The repetition of the first person personal pronoun here underscores the adversarial relationship between Prometheus and the gods, the separation between the divine and human spheres. Although the ode is structured as a dialogue between Prometheus and Jupiter, Jupiter's voice is missing, his refusal to reply indicative of the god's lack of compassion for humanity. The sole voice of the poem is that of Prometheus, and it acquires a monumental stature in its solitary defiance of the king of the gods:

> I pay homage to you? For what?
> Have you ever relieved
> The burdened man's anguish?
> Have you ever assuaged
> The frightened man's tears?
>
> (37–41)

The rebellious Titan thus belittles the god's absent authority, emphasizing both the intense suffering of mankind and Jupiter's systematic refusal to alleviate it. In this way Goethe presents Prometheus taking a strong stand in the battle between gods and humans on behalf of the latter. As Carl Kerényi argues, Prometheus functions here not as a god himself but rather as 'the immortal prototype of man as the original rebel and affirmer of his fate' (Kerényi 1963: 17). While the gods are uncaring, silent and indifferent to human suffering, Prometheus has modelled man's existence on his own. The poem concludes:

> Here I sit, forming men
> In my image,
> A race to resemble me:
> To suffer, to weep,
> To enjoy, to be glad –
> And never to heed you,
> Like me!
>
> (51–57)

Goethe's Prometheus thus creates mankind in his own likeness ('a race to resemble me'), invoking his own mixed experiences to illuminate the inherent duality of the human experience. Humans both weep and feel delight. Goethe's Prometheus defies the gods, and he serves as a model for a rebellious human race as well. Like Goethe's Faust,

Figure 7 School of Maso Finiguerra (1426–64), *Prometheus*, c. 1470–75. Pen and brown ink and brown wash over black chalk

Source: Copyright the British Museum. Presented by the Ruskin Museum, Sheffield

Prometheus does not quail at the absence of gods, but rather embraces this autonomous existence, for he has the power to create in his own image. Prometheus expresses the divine creative power inherent in human beings, and in this respect, the poem, called by one critic 'perhaps the most self-centered text of German literary history', is also very much about Goethe's own poetic genius – his own artistic identity, his ability to create himself through his poetry. The poem, after all, ends with the first-person pronoun (*Ich*); it first enables and then celebrates Goethe's self-assertive subjectivity. Through Prometheus, Goethe's humans, indeed Goethe himself, can partake in the creative process – and that, perhaps, is the ultimate act of rebellion.

THE POLITICAL PROMETHEUS

Goethe's celebration of Prometheus as a model for the creativity of the individual artist is very much consonant with the themes of the Romantic movement; indeed, as we will see, other Romantic poets also embraced Prometheus' creative powers. His disengagement from politics after the revolutionary period, however, distinguished him from those British Romantic poets and writers who saw in Prometheus a powerful model for revolutionary change and rebellion. Indeed, in England towards the end of the eighteenth century, poets turned away from Prometheus, the creator of mankind, and focussed instead on his act of rebellion. In particular, as a model of resistance to divine tyranny and a powerful symbol of suffering, Prometheus offered a way to think about the complexities of a tumultuous political world. Poets like Shelley and Byron saw their lives transformed by the events of 1789–93. Inspired by the possibilities of overthrowing Europe's old monarchic regime, they applauded the transgressive potential of the French Revolution – soon tyranny would cease, and all would be truly free. Inevitably, however, appalled by revolutionary terror and Napoleonic despotism, they came to mistrust violent revolt, and Prometheus helped these poets think about the unintended consequences of rebellion as well – despotism, slavery, and human suffering.

Among English poets, the popularity of Prometheus is explained in part by the fact that translations of Aeschylus had recently made his myth more readily available to an English audience. T. Morrell's *Prometheus in Chains* (1773) was the first appearance of an Aeschylean play in English, and in 1777 Richard Potter presented the whole corpus in prose. The *Prometheus Bound* held a privileged position among Aeschylus' plays, reflecting, perhaps, its relevance to those political realities (tyranny and suffering) of the end of the eighteenth and early nineteenth centuries, especially the Napoleonic wars.

The inherently political nature of Prometheus' story as Aeschylus explored it was particularly attractive to the Romantic poets and revolutionary figures of this time. The flexibility of his myth helped them think about different political strategies in the face of power inequities: revolution or resistance, resigned deference or utopian imagination. In particular, Prometheus as political icon helped reconfigure notions of authority. Whether as a symbol of rebellion against tyrannical authority, the benefactor of mankind, or the very image of human suffering, Prometheus was central to the human political experience of the Romantic period.

Lord Byron (1788–1824) looked to Prometheus as a symbol of heroic individualism at odds with tyrannical powers both human and divine. At least seventeen allusions to Prometheus have been found in his works. As a young boy at Harrow School in England, Byron received an extensive literary education including composition exercises in Greek and Latin poetry, and in 1804, he set to verse a choral passage from Aeschylus' *Prometheus Bound*. Byron wrote that he 'was passionately fond as a boy' of Aeschylus' dramatic treatment of the Prometheus myth, and the play serves as the starting point for his own use of the myth to explore the political events of his day. In fact, most of Byron's rebels are Promethean; they risk all for forbidden knowledge and inspiration, freedom or power. Like Goethe, Byron invokes Prometheus' creative powers as a model for the powers and the sufferings of the poet who aims at eternal fame, seeking to be

> the new Prometheus of new men,
> Bestowing fire from heaven, and then, too late,
> Finding the pleasure given repaid with pain.
> > (*The Prophecy of Dante*, IV 14–16)

For Byron, Prometheus' punishment at the claws of the eagle offered an extreme example of his own suffering as poet at the hands of an unappreciative public.

Byron's *Ode to Prometheus* (1816) opens with a passionate address to the god, who alone took pity on mankind's suffering:

> Titan! To whose immortal eyes
>   The sufferings of mortality
>   Seen in their sad reality,
> Were not as things that gods despise;
> What was thy pity's recompense? (1–5)

What, Byron asks, did Prometheus get in return for his compassionate efforts on behalf of mankind? The unequivocal answer comes just two lines later: 'The rock, the vulture, and the chain.' The second stanza then heaps blame upon the forces that have punished Prometheus for helping mankind:

> Titan! to thee the strife was given
>   Between the suffering and the will,
>   Which torture where they cannot kill;
> And the inexorable heaven,
> And the deaf tyranny of Fate,
> The ruling principle of Hate,
> Which for its pleasure doth create
> The things it may annihilate,
> Refused thee even the boon to die;
> The wretched gift eternity
> Was thine – and thou hast borne it well.
>
>   (15–25)

Byron is working very much in the footsteps of Aeschylus, celebrating Prometheus' tireless endurance of all that the tyrannical forces of Zeus can dish out ('deaf tyranny of Fate') as well as his refusal to give in to 'the ruling principle of Hate'. For Byron, Prometheus' crime was to be kind: to try to lessen the suffering of mankind, the Titan dared stand up against an all powerful Zeus. In spite of his own suffering from the heavens, Prometheus continues with patience, endurance, and an 'impenetrable Spirit /Which Earth and Heaven could not convulse' (42–43).

These are the Promethean qualities of resistance and endurance that Byron holds up as 'a symbol and a sign' for mankind:

> Like thee, Man is in part divine,
> A troubled stream from a pure source;
> And Man in portions can foresee
> His own funereal destiny;
> His wretchedness, and his resistance,
> And his sad unallied existence . . .
>
> (47–52)

For Byron, Prometheus embodies the essence of the human experience – doomed to 'his own funeral destiny' yet possessed of a spirit of defiance that is equal to all suffering. Even with Prometheus' patronage, man can only defy the limitations posed by the loss of the Golden Age. And so, in the end mankind is still left in its 'sad unallied existence'. Byron's Prometheus offers no alternative to the suffering and endurance that marks the human experience. Instead, his story lends mythic stature to the necessary defiance against the terrible trinity of heaven, tyranny, and Fate, making in the end 'Death a Victory' (59). Byron's *Ode to Prometheus* utters a strong protest against injustice all the while it celebrates the Titan – and, by extension, all others (including himself) who dare defy the vultures to the end.

Byron wrote his *Ode to Prometheus* in Switzerland in July 1816 while in the company of Percy Bysshe Shelley, who was himself already thinking about his own Promethean poem. The two poets, together with Shelley's wife, Mary, spent the entire summer together on the shores of Lake Geneva, and, as Mary Shelley records, 'many and long were the conversations between Lord Byron and Shelley'. Shelley, himself, notes in his journal that the passage through the Alps brought Aeschylus' Prometheus play, set in the Caucasus mountains, to mind. The contemporary significance of Prometheus must have been a topic of discussion with the two poets, each of whom looked to the mythic figure as a way to think about man's place in the early nineteenth-century political scene. They both rejected the excesses of tyranny and sympathized with oppressed peoples, and they both looked to Prometheus to articulate responses to the political situation, and yet each with very different results. Where Byron focusses on the oppressive tyrannical policies of those in power, celebrating the human experience of resistance and suffering, Shelley dismantles the opposition of Prometheus and Jupiter to expand his utopian vision of love and non-defiance.

SHELLEY'S *PROMETHEUS UNBOUND* AND THE POWER OF LOVE

Percy Bysshe Shelley (1792–1822) came of age during the height of the Napoleonic Wars and rebelled from his aristocratic roots on several levels, political and religious. A public declaration of atheism got him expelled from Oxford, an event which, combined with his associations with utopian and other radical groups, no doubt contributed to his alienation from his father. The *Prometheus Unbound* is the last of three long dramatic poems that Shelley wrote on religious and political despotism of the early nineteenth century. The poem symbolizes not just a revolutionary triumph over authoritarian rule, but the deliverance of mankind from oppression, both political and religious, into a more harmonious and loving relationship with nature.

In the *Prometheus Unbound*, Shelley's revised Prometheus offers hope as the key to the salvation of humanity. Written in 1818–19 and published in 1820, the *Prometheus Unbound* was one of Shelley's favourite works. Shelley's Prometheus is still a hero of human liberation, clearly endebted to Aeschylus' defiant Titan who opposed the harsh tyranny of Zeus on behalf of mankind. And yet, he departs from Aeschylus' model in some significant ways. From the perspective of thirty-thousand years of torture, Shelley's Prometheus has seen the error of his hateful ways, and his rebellion is a thing of the past. He no longer wishes for revenge; he seeks no power for himself. Instead of the revolutionary power and technological potential of Aeschylus or the rebellious defiance of Byron, the new Promethean fire is the liberating power of love which can transform the human condition. Shelley offers this radical rereading of Aeschylus' lost play of the same name by complicating the familiar adversarial categories of rebel and tyrant. Although his choice of title clearly acknowledges Aeschylus' trilogy, Shelley explains in his preface that his ambition is greater than to restore the lost play. Instead, he re-imagines the conclusion to the Prometheus/Jupiter conflict at the heart of the myth, wanting to avoid 'a catastrophe so feeble as that of reconciling the Champion with the Oppressor of mankind'.

One specific way that Shelley rehabilitates the Promethean figures of his predecessors is by setting the action of his story years after the initial act of rebellion. The focus thus shifts from the conflict between tyrant and rebel to a more idealistic and constructive model for life without any tyrannical constraints – political, intellectual, or religious. And so Shelley's Prometheus is more about imagining an escape from the institution of tyranny than a lament on its limitations. Redeemed by many years of suffering, Shelley's Prometheus has become 'the type of the highest perfection of moral and intellectual nature, impelled by the purest and the truest motives to the best and noblest ends'.

As the work opens, Prometheus appears 'nailed to this wall of eagle-baffling mountain' (1.20) in Indian Caucasus, the cradle of civilization and evocative of the new world imagination of the play. Prometheus has endured thirty thousand years of torture by Jupiter, and yet he still remains defiant. The action of the drama is quite minimal: it begins with Prometheus' denunciation of Jupiter whose reign has filled men 'With fear and self-contempt and barren hope'. He is defiant yet has come to suggest a new way to resist tyranny. Shelley's Prometheus conjures up the Phantasm of Jupiter to repeat his curse against the authoritarian god before then recalling it. Prometheus himself has seen the error of his earlier hatred and desire for vengeance and wishes 'no living thing to suffer pain' (1.1.305)' – not even Jupiter. When Mercury calls up the Furies to tempt Prometheus into despair, Prometheus resists and puts all his faith in the power of love: 'I said all hope was vain but love' (1.824).

Asia, Prometheus' wife and feminine counterpart in Shelley's version, dominates the second act in which Shelley rewrites the Hesiodic narrative of the ages of mankind. Toward the end of the act, Asia goes to the cave of Demogorgon – a dark and problematic figure whom Harold Bloom calls 'a demonic parody of the Spirit' – where the two converse on the creation of the living world and the ages of man. First was the Golden Age, where man's happiness was immature and incomplete. Then, Jupiter came to power, and Prometheus 'clothed him with the dominion of wide Heaven' enjoining him to "let man be free" (2.4.45–46). But with the reign of Jupiter, man's suffering and strife began, and Prometheus intervened and 'waked the legioned hopes' of mankind for which, as the myth inevitably goes, he was punished by Jupiter.

In the third act Jupiter falls into the abyss at the hands of Demogorgon, and Hercules unbinds Prometheus and restores him to Asia – thus introducing Shelley's vision of a return to the Golden Age in which 'thrones were kingless, and men walked/ one with other even as spirits do' (3.4.131–32). The final act, then, celebrates the power of human love 'which makes all it gazes on, paradise' (4.128). The chorus of spirits proclaim:

> We will take our plan
> From the new world of man,
> And our work shall be called the Promethean.
>
> (4.156–58)

As Shelley explains in the Preface, his imagery was 'drawn from the operations of the human mind', and while the action of the play may be simple, the ideas involved are quite complex. For Shelley, the oppositional categories that have dominated political thought are overly simplistic, and the ambiguous richness of the Prometheus myth allows him to rethink them. Shelley's Prometheus revisits recent historical events and describes a better outcome, moving beyond the cycles of revolution to a vision of a world without 'thrones, altars, judgement-seats, and prisons' (3.4.164). In this new world, these and other trappings of power, fear, and hatred 'stand, not o'erthrown, but unregarded now' (3.4.179).

The age-old categories of tyrant and rebel, master and slave are no longer entrenched through the timeless opposition of Prometheus and Jupiter; rather they begin to collapse into each other. Certainly, Jupiter is presented as the all-powerful tyrant. He glories in the fact that his empire is built upon 'Hell's coeval, fear' (3.1.10). His punishments are unduly harsh, and yet, Shelley's Jupiter is also a slave – a slave to evil. As Demogorgon explains, 'All spirits are enslaved who serve things evil' (2.4.110). In this respect, Shelley was in line with other political theorists of his day who saw tyranny itself as a kind of slavery – tyrants were governed by their insatiable greed, hatred, and evil, and had lost control of their better selves. Along these same lines, Shelley also portrays Jupiter as a kind of rebel. For not only did Jupiter, after all, rise to power through rebellion, slaying his father to set up one tyranny in exchange for another, but to set oneself up as supreme ruler is itself an act of rebellion against the common will, and Shelley thus establishes Jupiter, not Prometheus, as the real rebel of the play.

For Prometheus, himself, has recanted his role as rebel together with his curse upon Jupiter:

> I speak in grief,
> Not exultation, for I hate no more
> As then, ere misery made me wise. The curse
> Once breathed on thee I would recall.
>
> (1.56–59)

Instead of representing the spirit of defiance in the *Prometheus Unbound*, Prometheus stands as the symbol for passive resistance, forgiveness, and love. By recalling the curse, Prometheus recognizes that he shares with Jupiter responsibility for the troubles at the beginning of the play. His own misjudgement makes him an accessory to Jupiter's tyranny, and guilty of bringing pain to humans. Shelley's Prometheus is implicated in Jupiter's tyranny because he was the one who gave Jupiter power without wisdom, and this error in judgement makes him guilty as well. While Jupiter remains a slave to his arrogance and his thirst for vengeance, Prometheus is liberated by recanting his curse. Shelley's drama thus resists Aeschylus' plan to resolve his trilogy by reconciling tyrant and rebel.

In addition to recasting the characters of Prometheus and Jupiter, Shelley reconceptualizes the role of mankind in the myth, emphasizing that it was not Jupiter who intended to thwart mankind, but that man was his own enslaver and liberator. Instead of advocating revolution, Shelly looks to Prometheus to imagine a way out of the endless cycle of tyranny. He aims to create a new Golden Age where men live in a state of political equality; each king of himself:

> Sceptreless, free, uncircumscribed – but man:
> Equal, unclassed, tribeless and nationless;

> Exempt from awe, worship, degree; the king
> Over himself; just, gentle, wise – but man:
>> (3.4.194–97)

Man thus becomes an autonomous agent, a player in his own story rather than the victim of political abuse or the recipient of divine patronage.

By reconfiguring the roles and relationships of the primary characters in the Prometheus myth – Prometheus, Jupiter, and mankind – Shelley exploits the mythological tradition to challenge the very assumption that a divine monarch offers the best model for the human political realm. Instead of celebrating Prometheus the rebel who overturns a harsh tyrant, as Byron does, or attempting to reconcile rebel and tyrant, as Aeschylus is thought to have done, Shelley sets out a blueprint for a new intellectual revolution in which the children of Prometheus release themselves from the authority of priest and king – in which man is 'king over himself'. Shelley devotes only four lines to Hercules' act of unbinding Prometheus, for that mythic rescue has been overshadowed by the significance of Prometheus' own action of recalling his curse. Shelley insists instead on the human capacity to change political destiny when he gives Prometheus the choice to renounce a vindictive cycle of revenge in favour of universal equality and harmony. Shelley replaces Byron's focus on Prometheus' defiance of Heaven, Fate, and Hate with the more idealistic principles of hope and love. Prometheus' change of mind enables a powerful change in the lives of those men for whom he is a symbol. Shelley rewrites the mythic tradition to advocate equality for all and to denounce violent revolutions completely. Violence only begets more violence, and mankind throws off the chains of tyranny rather than those of a specific tyrant.

PROMETHEUS AND NAPOLEON

The myth of Prometheus, with its ambiguous complexity and its focus on the use and abuse of power, was particularly resonant for those poets trying to come to grips with the larger-than-life figure of

THE MODERN PROMETHEUS, OR DOWNFALL OF TYRANNY.
This Print Presented gratis to every Purchaser of a Ticket or Share at Martins Lottery Office & Cornhill

Figure 8 George Cruikshank, *The Modern Prometheus, or Downfall of Tyranny*, London 1814

Source: Copyright the British Museum

Napoleon, the 27-year-old champion of humanity who seized the revolution and set out to control the destiny of nations. It is perhaps with Napoleon in mind that Shelley's *Prometheus Unbound* addresses the fine line between rebel, liberator, and tyrant – spelling out the dangers of both the *ancien régime* and the Napoleonic Empire. As one scholar notes,

> to look at the hopes with which the Revolution began, to see them then transformed into the Roman trappings of Napoleon replete with martial eagles as icons, and then to watch them dashed on the rocks of St. Helena, that is to contemplate Prometheus and discover in his image the Phantasm of Jupiter.
>
> (Curran 1986: 446)

The Romantic poets invoked a range of different Napoleons as a crucial part of their sustained and partisan engagement with the political and cultural issues of their times. They lionized him, they appropriated him as a figure of power, and they demonized him – all in their efforts to declare their political positions as well as to articulate their self-conceptions and roles as poets. For Napoleon was the supreme embodiment of a hero in an age in which the artist as well was increasingly seen as heroic. Aspects of Napoleon's genius – his energy, imagination, and daring – were also qualities that poets and writers of the time liked to attribute to themselves, and the figure of Napoleon was thus drawn into a crucial Romantic debate over the relative value of poetic and political power. In grappling with the complexities and contradictions of the dynamic public figure of Napoleon in their poetry, the Romantics looked to a host of historical and mythical analogies, including, predictably, Prometheus.

Byron's *Ode to Napoleon Bonaparte*, for example, written upon the ruler's abdication in 1814, invokes Prometheus in an attempt to restore the poet's faith in Napoleon. The ode is full of tensions and conflicting imagery as Byron alternately inflates and deflates Napoleon. He casts Napoleon's fall from power in epic terms with an epigram from Gibbon's *Rise and Fall of the Roman Empire*, and yet he attempts to salvage some of the emperor's mythic force by representing the defeated commander imprisoned on Elba as a mighty Titan chained to his rock in Caucasus. The poem opens with a harsh expression of the poet's bitter disillusionment, but Byron summons up his admiration for the fallen ruler in the final stanza of the Ode, comparing Napoleon to Prometheus, defiant at the end:

> Or like the thief of fire from heaven,
>   Wilt thou withstand the shock?
> And share with him, the unforgiven,
>   His vulture and his rock!
> Foredoomed by God – by man accurst,
> And that last act, though not thy worst,
>   The very Fiend's arch mock;
> He in his fall preserv'd his pride,
> And if a mortal, had as proudly died!
>
>   (136–44)

Some see the ode as an attack on Napoleon for a failure of the Promethean spirit – for forsaking his principles of liberty and freedom in a search for personal power and glory. Others see the opposite, suggesting that Byron here sketches out a new heroic role for Napoleon – and, by extension, himself. By transforming Napoleon into a Promethean figure, Byron associates the fallen ruler with liberty and defiance, and implies his ultimate triumph. Byron offers Napoleon the possibility of Promethean status by rewriting his act of surrender as one of defiance. It is possible to see Byron's attempts here to redeem Napoleon as a symbol of strength as a strategy of self redefinition as well. As Byron evaluates his place in a society from which he feels alienated, he turns to Napoleon's abdication from the world stage to help clarify his own identity as poet.

Upon Napoleon's death in 1821, the poet and artist, William Blake, painted the emperor as a Promethean figure in *The Spiritual Form of Napoleon*. While the painting no longer exists, it was described in 1876 as portraying Napoleon as a 'strong energetic figure grasping at the sun and moon with his hands, yet chained to earth by one foot, and with a pavement of dead bodies before him in the foreground'. Blake had brought together the fortunes of Napoleon at the level of historical allegory in his epics as well: Blake's Prometheus figure, Orc, had risen up against the sky-god figure Urizen much as Napoleon had become transformed into yet another tyrant figure. In part because of his fascination with strong personality of genius, Goethe also remained to the end an admirer of Napoleon, despite Napoleon's dismantling of the Empire and old regime in Germany. The mythic range and potential of Prometheus was particularly well-suited to the issues close to the heart of the Romantic poets and artists. Napoleon's role on the world stage was a complex one – as bringer of hope and suffering, as revolutionary turned emperor – and the mythic persona of Prometheus was an important part of many representations of Napoleon in the public imaginary.

FRANKENSTEIN, OR THE MODERN PROMETHEUS

In the *Prometheus Unbound*, Shelley uses Prometheus to help undo the myth of patriarchal power, both theoretically and as recently embodied by the historical figure of Napoleon. For Shelley, this political act is fundamentally one of the imagination, for, as he claims, 'poets are the unacknowledged legislators of the world'. The symbolism of Shelley's *Prometheus Unbound* operates at a level beyond politics as well, invoking the image of Prometheus' liberation from Jupiter's chains to represent the forces in man's soul that combine to release his creative power and restore his imaginative freedom. As we saw in our discussion of Goethe, Prometheus serves as a powerful symbol of the imagination's ability to break the chains of inherited myths and the familiar habits of imagining the world and man's place in it. For many Romantic poets, Prometheus' story fuelled the imaginative arts, elaborating a vision of the rebellious yet creative poet/artist – the ultimate fire thief.

Perhaps the definitive treatment of the creative aspect of the Prometheus myth is Mary Shelley's *Frankenstein* (subtitled 'The Modern Prometheus'), and I will conclude this chapter by revisiting this theme through the distorted lens of Mary Shelley's Gothic novel, for she offers the greatest testament to the creative power of the Prometheus myth even as she calls it into question. Mary Wollstonecraft Shelley (1797–1851) was the daughter of two distinguished literary celebrities, William Godwin and Mary Wollstonecraft (who died soon after giving birth to her daughter). She received an excellent education at home in the company of her father's intellectual friends and expected herself to become a writer like both her parents. Mary met Percy Shelley, a student of her father's, in 1812 and eloped with him to France two years later. After several difficult years, Mary Shelley accompanied her husband to Switzerland, where they met Byron, and it was there that she conceived the idea for writing her most famous novel on the horrific consequences of a scientific experiment gone wrong. Responding to Byron's challenge that they each write a ghost story, Mary Shelley began work on a manuscript that was first published anonymously in 1818 as *Frankenstein, or The Modern Prometheus*. A new edition, revised by Mary Shelley, appeared in 1831.

Mary Shelley explains that she was prompted to write her 'ghost story' after listening to hours of talk on the 'principle of life' by her husband and Byron. Their graphic speculations about various strategies for reanimating corpses were transformed through her vivid imagination into a gripping novel about the power of invention to 'give form to dark, shapeless, substances'. Like others before her, Mary Shelley looked to Prometheus, the mythic creator of humans to explore questions about the nature and possibilities of creation. One likely source of inspiration was the English philosopher and politician Lord Shaftesbury, whose 1709 work *The Moralists* includes numerous references to Prometheus as the original creator of mankind in ways that suggest a direct connection with some ideas in *Frankenstein*. For example, he holds Prometheus responsible for mankind's imperfections:

who with thy stol'n Celestial Fire, mix'd with vile Clay, dids't mock Heaven's Countenance, and in abusive Likeness of the Immortals, mad'st the Compound Man; that wretched Mortal, ill to himself, and Cause of Ill to all.

(Cited in Small 1972: 51)

A person of significant culture and education, Mary Shelley may also have read Goethe's Prometheus poems or seen Beethoven's 1801 ballet *The Creatures of Prometheus* performed in Vienna. By contrast to her husband, Mary Shelley looked to the creative aspects of Prometheus' persona to ask important questions about the limits of the artistic and scientific imagination.

In addition to its fascination with political issues, the end of the eighteenth century was a time of scientific optimism, and Mary Shelley set her modern Prometheus story in the workshop of a scientist whose far-reaching ambitions lead him to create life only to discover that his creature has a mind of its own. The novel is comprised of three interlocking stories, each with its own narrator, all three of whom are explorers of the human race and its environment. The first narrator is Walton, a would-be Arctic explorer who writes to his sister as he prepares to join an expedition to the North Pole. His ship is stranded, surrounded by ice, and the sailors bring aboard a man in a state of exhaustion who recognizes in Walton a kindred spirit and tells him his own cautionary tale.

This second narrator is Victor Frankenstein, and he tells Walton how he, driven by a desire to learn 'the secrets of heaven and earth', discovered how to create life. After many long nights in his laboratory, Frankenstein admits that as soon as he gave life to his creation (unnamed and usually referred to as the Monster or the Fiend), he was immediately repulsed by his results and fled. The monster disappeared, too, but soon Frankenstein explains that he learned that his infant brother had been murdered. Returning home, he caught a glimpse of the Monster and suspected, correctly, that he was responsible for his brother's death. Eventually the two met face to face on a glacier at Chamonix, and the Monster compelled his creator to listen to his story.

The monster himself thus takes up the role of narrator at this point in the novel and tells his version of his own creation. With incredible self-awareness, he recounts the story of his gradual growth and development, due, in part, to his astute observation of a family whom he observed through a crack in the wall. He became attached to the family, he explains, but when he approached them, they, too, rejected him. Further embittered, he travelled to Geneva, where he saw a young boy and captured him, intending to 'educate him as my companion and friend'. When he discovered that the boy was his creator's younger brother, he killed him in a rage. At this point in his story, the monster turns to Frankenstein and appealing to his sense of justice, entreats him to make a female creature for him, promising that with such a companion, he would flee human society and live in the most savage of places, hurting no one. Reluctantly Frankenstein agrees to make a female monster, but then, taking up his story again, Frankenstein explains that he changed his mind at the last minute, fearing that such a union would produce a monstrous race. The Monster got his revenge by killing first Frankenstein's best friend and then by strangling his creator's bride on their wedding night. Frankenstein recounts how he set off in pursuit of the Monster into the Arctic, where Walton found and rescued him, promising to take up his task of destroying the Monster.

The novel concludes with the resumption of Walton's narrative – he recounts his growing friendship with Frankenstein and the increasing danger of his Arctic expedition. He describes the death of Frankenstein and the final appearance of the Monster who had come to mourn the death of his creator. The Monster then departs into the Arctic darkness, promising to destroy himself.

While the novel is very much a product of its times, responding to both the horrors of the French Revolution and the promises of scientific exploration, it retains its power for us even today because so many of the questions it raises still haunt us. The unnamed Monster serves as a complicated symbol of the many fears that lie below the surface of civilization – war, violence, oppression – as well as of the basic human need for love and affection. But above all, the novel raises enduring Promethean questions about the dangers of unbridled scientific research and the limitations of the creative process – what are the moral issues involved when mankind metaphorically steals fire and usurps the divine power of creation?

Again, it is precisely the ambiguous nature of the mythic figure Prometheus that helps Mary Shelley address these problematic issues located in the creative process. Who is the creator? Who is the creature? What is their relationship to each other? At first, it seems clear that there are many Promethean qualities to Victor Frankenstein. He wants to be a benefactor of mankind; in his scientific researches he rebels against the established order, and he steals, as it were, the power from heaven to create a human being. As he explains, 'With an anxiety that almost amounted to agony, I collected the instruments of life around me, that I might infuse a spark of being into the lifeless thing that lay at my feet' (38). And, like Prometheus, when Frankenstein finally does succeed in creating new life, his monstrous creation brings death and destruction to all those he tried to help.

At the same time, the monster exhibits some Promethean qualities of his own. He discovers fire; like Aeschylus' Prometheus, he knows a secret about a wedding that threatens to undo his master; and he is condemned to a life not asked for, suffering at the hands of his creator. Even more interesting, the story that the monster recounts to Frankenstein when they first meet face to face is a very Promethean one – it articulates the stages of man's progress from a bestial existence thanks to Prometheus' gifts to mankind.

When he first escaped from Frankenstein's laboratory, the monster tells his creator, he was forced to wander alone in the wilderness, eating raw berries from the ground and drinking from a brook. Barely clad in some rags, he says of himself: 'I was a poor, helpless, miserable wretch' (80). Although he slowly acquires first the elementary five senses and then a sense of pleasure and wonder, he explains that he was still intellectually undeveloped: 'No distinct ideas occupied my mind; all was confused' (80). His narrative closely echoes the speech of Aeschylus' Prometheus that described men in much the same terms before his intervention:

> For men first had eyes but could not see; they had ears but could not hear; instead; like the shapes of dreams they conducted all matters in confusion for their whole long life . . . they lived like swarming ants in the sunless hollows of caves.
>
> (Aeschylus, *Prometheus Bound* 447–53)

Shelley's Monster explains that he, too, wandered among nature, really at one with it, until one cold night he discovered a fire that had been left by some wandering beggars (81). Impressed by its heat, he soon learned to make a fire of his own, and subsequently to cook food instead of eating it raw. Next, he discovered the advantages of shelter from the elements, and like the men in Protagoras' Prometheus myth, learned that humans can live together more profitably in larger groups. His subsequent education and socialization again follows very much in the footsteps of Aeschylus' Prometheus, who extends his gift of fire and technology to encompass all forms of learning and arts as well.

In short, this extended narrative of the Monster's first days can be read as an allegorical account of man's evolutionary progress. More specifically, it reprises the story of human development and progress as detailed through the myth of Prometheus in Aeschylus' *Prometheus Bound* and in Plato's *Protagoras*. Although the Monster is prevented from making the ultimate transformation from beast to civilized man, his narrative indicates his awareness of what it takes (education, socialization, love) to become truly human – as well as of his own failings in that direction. If Frankenstein mimics Prometheus' rebellious act of creating humans, the Monster embodies the Promethean narrative of mankind's progress. And yet – and this is Mary Shelley's macabre twist on the myth – neither one is entirely successful.

It should come as no surprise that both Frankenstein and the monster exhibit Promethean qualities given the tensions at the heart of the Promethean myth itself. The complexity of Prometheus' persona – both creator and saviour of mankind and symbol of its suffering – enables a kind of moral ambiguity that distinguishes Mary Shelley's novel from the work of other Romantic authors who celebrate Prometheus' creative powers. Whereas in her husband's *Prometheus Unbound*, a totally pure and noble Promethean figure helps recreate a free and classless human condition, in *Frankenstein*, both creator and creature are identified with Prometheus, and neither one of them is morally pure. The novel explores the exhilarating sense of power, the ability to break barriers that accompanies the actions of the creator even as it sympathizes with the feelings of impotence and isolation that belong to the creature. Moreover, over the course of the novel, both creator and creature, Frankenstein and the Monster, merge into one another. The Monster becomes the tyrant, a creator of death, and lords his destructive power over his master, while Frankenstein has become the slave of his creature and suffers at his hands.

What emerges from the novel's use of Promethean imagery is a complex critique of the Romantic notion of creativity. In Mary Shelley's *Frankenstein*, the creative force, as symbolized through Prometheus, is dangerous and unpredictable. There is an obsessive possessiveness to Frankenstein's motives as scientific creator that undercuts his allegedly pure motives of benefaction. What starts off as an act of generosity soon turns into one of control. Later we find that his extreme devotion to his scientific research leads Frankenstein to reject normal society, to ignore friends and family, and work fanatically in a dark and dreary workshop. It comes as little surprise, then, that the scientist working under such conditions, and with materials furnished from the dissecting room and the slaughterhouse, is repulsed when confronted by the fruits of his creative efforts. He explains: 'Unable to endure the aspect of the being I had created, I rushed out of the room . . .' (39).

Frankenstein's act of creation is thus fraught with the potential of monstrosity. Combined with the Monster's self-conscious reflections on his failures as a human, Frankenstein's 'scientific' research raises important questions about the limits to the creative process and the need for some sense of moral responsibility that, as we will see in the next chapter, continue to challenge creative scientific projects in the twenty-first century. Mary Shelley's meditation on the creative process reveals the dark underside to the visionary dreams of remaking man that fuelled the imagination of Romantic mythmakers. She challenges those who looked to Prometheus to celebrate and valorize the role of the isolated, creative artist, suggesting that the worst thing is for the artist to let his own power as creator outweigh his commitment to humanity.

Whereas Goethe and Byron invoke Prometheus to celebrate the poet's creative powers, Mary Shelley hones in on the problematic potential of the creative spirit itself – its often obsessive, tyrannical side. Mary Shelley looks to Prometheus to combine two images that are at the very core of the Romantic vision. With the monster, she evokes Prometheus as the symbol of man as suffering creature while with Frankenstein, she conjures up images of man as a powerful creator. By collapsing the suffering creature into the all-powerful creator, she turns the Romantic myth of creativity back upon itself to produce what Paul Cantor calls the 'nightmare of romantic idealism'.

OVERVIEW

Hans Blumenberg, in his *Work on Myth*, argues that at the core of Prometheus' story is the fundamental myth of privation of power in which Prometheus figures as symbol of hope for mankind. Certainly for the British Romantic poets, Byron and Shelley, still processing the political promises and disasters of the French Revolution, the Prometheus myth was an extremely useful conceptual tool to re-imagine power relations and the human condition. For Goethe and Mary Shelley, on the other hand, Prometheus' creative powers, his role as the creator of mankind, served as a productive point of departure for meditations on the creative process – both its powers and its limitations. As the thief of fire from the heavens, Prometheus symbolized all humans striving for political power and self-rule; as the bringer of light, he represented humans breaking free of constraints – political, moral, and religious. As saviour, he stood as icon of hope for the perfectability of mankind, while as creator, he celebrates mankind's power to give life and to remake the world as a better place for all.

5

PROMETHEUS IN THE CONTEMPORARY AGE

In this concluding chapter, we turn to Prometheus in the twentieth century. It should come as no great surprise that in an age dominated by digital technology, extraordinary life-extending medical and scientific breakthroughs, and incessant technological innovation that Prometheus continues to loom large in the collective psyche. What are the themes and issues that emerge from a twentieth-century Prometheus? Does Prometheus tell an Aeschylean tale of progress or a Hesiodic story of decline? Do the political issues that were so important to the Romantic notion of Prometheus still have purchase in the late twentieth century? Does Prometheus still symbolize the creative impulse? A close look at the British poet and playwright Tony Harrison's movie *Prometheus* (1998) will show that the answer to all of these questions is a resounding yes. Harrison's movie is set in northern England amidst a coal miners' strike and isolates technology, work, and artistic creation as three key themes of the twentieth-century Prometheus. In addition, Harrison works back through Shelley's *Prometheus Unbound* to offer a Hesiodic twist on Aeschylus' more optimistic treatment of the Titan's myth. Hence his movie will give us an opportunity to reflect on the themes we have highlighted in previous chapters of this book.

PROMETHEUS IN THE ARTS

Throughout the twentieth century, composers and choreographers, visual artists, playwrights, and directors continued to look to Prometheus to help describe what is means to be human. Consider first the fields of music and dance. In 1909, the Russian Alexander Scriabin, sometimes considered the first contemporary composer, wrote a symphony entitled *Prometheus* or *Poem of Fire*. Now, at the beginning of the twenty-first century, Prometheus lends his name to a company, Prometheus Music, that specializes in music about space exploration, science-fiction, and fantasy. In dance, Ninette de Valois, founder and director of the Royal Ballet, choreographed a

Figure 9 José Clemente Orozco, *Prometheus*, 1930. Fresco mural, Pomona College, Claremont, CA

Source: Photo courtesy of Pomona College Museum of Art

ballet *Prometheus*, using the music by Beethoven, which was first performed in 1936 at Sadler's Wells. In 1970, her associate and successor, Frederick Ashton choreographed *The Creatures of Prometheus* with music by John Lanchbery (after Beethoven) first performed in Bonn. Today, Prometheus gives his name to one of Massachusetts' leading modern dance companies.

In the visual arts, Maxfield Parrish's Prometheus appeared in the General Electric Mazda lamps calendar in 1919. In 1930 the Mexican muralist José Clemente Orozco painted a monumental Prometheus mural in the Refectory at Pomona College (Fig. 9). Orozco's Prometheus is caught in the act of stealing fire, situated in the midst of a divided sea of humanity – some embracing his gift, some turning away in fear. Paul Manship was commissioned in 1933 to create a gilded bronze fountain sculpture of Prometheus proudly holding his torch aloft in the newly built Rockefeller Center as part of the Center's broader theme of 'New Frontiers and the March of Civilization' (Fig. 10). In 1936 Jacques Lipchitz's sculpture 'Prometheus Strangling the Vulture' was exhibited at the Paris World Fair (Fig. 11). Prometheus stealing the fire also captured the imagination of the British artist Peter De Francia in a 1982 drawing on paper (Fig. 12). In 1999, the multimedia artist Mark Wallinger created a projected video installation entitled *Prometheus* that transports Prometheus's eternal punishment in the twentieth century through endlessly repeated videos of the artist seated in an electric chair.

Prometheus has made several appearances on stage as well. In 1927, a group of Greek intellectuals and nationalists in New York, known as the Delphic Circle, staged Aeschylus' *Prometheus Bound* in Delphi as part of a larger utopian vision of intellectual aristocracy and world peace. In 1967, Jonathan Miller directed Robert Lowell's prose adaptation of Aeschylus' *Prometheus Bound* at the Yale Repertory Theater, set in a context which evoked the Spanish Inquisition to link the tyranny of Zeus with other authoritarian regimes. In 1968, Carl Orff's opera *Prometheus* was produced in Munich with enlarged images of Prometheus' face projected onto the rock on which the Titan was impaled, and in 1989, Tom Paulin was commissioned by the BBC to produce a Prometheus play as part of an Open University course on fifth-century Athens and democracy. Paulin set out to translate the

Figure 10 Paul Manship, *Prometheus*, 1933. Rockefeller Center, New York

Source: Photo courtesy of David Hay

political themes of Aeschylus' play into a contemporary idiom, rooted in the discourse of protest in the twentieth century. The flexibility of the Promethean narrative continues to provide contemporary artists with a rich mythic canvas on which to paint a twentieth-century portrait of the human condition.

THE MOST PROMETHEAN OF THE PROMETHEANS: BREAKTHROUGHS IN SCIENCE AND TECHNOLOGY

Prometheus has helped shape the scientific and technological vision of the twentieth century as well. A moon of Saturn, a mountain in Nevada, and a host of professional journals and Internet sites are all

Figure 11 Jacques Lipchitz, *Prometheus, Strangling the Vulture*, 1949

Source: Philadelphia Museum of Art: purchased with the Lisa Norris Elkins Fund

Figure 12 Peter De Francia, *Prometheus Steals the Fire*
Source: Tate, London 2004

named after Prometheus. David Landes, one of the most influential historians of the industrial revolution, celebrated the 'new age of promise' brought on by the technological innovations of the late nineteenth century in a book appropriately entitled *The Unbound Prometheus* (1969). At the dawn of the twentieth century, Prometheus lent his name to a German trade magazine for industrial technology (*Prometheus: Illustrated Weekly on Developments in Trade, Industry, and Science*, Leipzig: 1899–1921), and now, in the early twenty-first century, as we embrace technological innovations in a variety of venues – medical, digital, scientific – Prometheus continues to embody our complex attitude towards technology.

In the field of medicine, for example, Prometheus symbolizes the many advances that the medical profession has made towards enhancing and prolonging – even creating – human life. A recent article in the *New England Journal of Medicine* looks to the myth of

Prometheus and his endlessly regenerative liver to introduce an article on the potential of stem-cell research: 'The Promethean promise of eternal regeneration awaits us while time's vulture looks on' (Rosenthal 2003). Prometheus Laboratories, a specialized pharmaceutical company located in San Diego, California, recalls Prometheus' inspiration for medical discovery in naming its lab and in defining its corporate missions as 'providing the information and tools necessary to treat patients throughout the healthcare continuum'.

If anything, in the age of digital technology, the appeal of the ancient myth of Prometheus has grown. With its unparalleled potential for the storage and dissemination of information around the globe, digital technology gives power and knowledge to individuals who might otherwise be socially excluded and politically marginalized. As Darin Barney puts it in a book on information technology and democracy, 'Prometheus is certainly unbound, but he is also wired' (Barney 2000: 6). Invoking Prometheus, John Perry Barlow, former Grateful Dead songwriter and co-founder of the electronic Frontier Foundation, characterizes the movement of digitized information over computer networks as 'the most profound technological shift since the capture of fire' (cited in Barney 2000: 4).

New developments in the pursuit of energy form part of the Promethean technological revolution as well. In recognition of the dramatic ability of the species to harness the energy of nuclear fission, Prometheus gives his name to 'promethium' (atomic number 61), a rare earth metal that is five hundred times 'hotter' than radium. As Robert De Ropp puts it in his book on *The New Prometheans*, pioneers in the field of atomic energy may be regarded as 'the most Promethean of the Prometheans'. He reminds us that in a very short period of time they transported humankind from one age into another: 'By releasing the power latent in the nucleus of the atom they made the theft of the original Prometheus seems like a very minor piece of effrontery' (De Ropp 1972: 1).

THE AMBIGUOUS PROMETHEAN LEGACY

And yet, on nearly every technological front, it is not just that we return to Prometheus in an unqualified celebration of the technological skills that his gift of fire made possible. Equally significant, the very ambiguity built into his story has inspired a parallel critique of the ever-growing use of technology in the twentieth and twenty-first centuries. Invoking Prometheus thus helps us think about both the benefits of technological inventions and about the dire threats they pose to humanity. In the wake of the Human Genome Project, experimentation in cloning, and our ever-growing bag of pharmaceutical tricks, the monstrous potential of genetic and reproductive technologies prompts us to revisit even more urgently the questions about the creative impulse and the role of science posed so graphically in Mary Shelley's *Frankenstein*.

Some turn to Epimetheus, Prometheus' dim-witted brother, to articulate the pessimistic strain of Prometheus' interventions – the fear that the unprecedented arrogance of human beings has irrevocably upset the balance of nature. De Ropp has argued that for every Promethean technological advance there has been a corresponding Epimethean lack of foresight that threatens to erase its potential benefits or worse. He marvels that these 'Epimetheans' have not yet succeeded in either blowing up the planet or letting loose a new plague against which humankind would be defenceless. De Ropp's worries seem ever more prescient in light of escalations in the tools and technology of terrorism at the beginning of the twenty-first century. As we become used to the new challenges of the twenty-first century, it is not a lack of expertise or material resources that impedes our progress in nearly every field of scientific and technological endeavour, but rather a sense of spiritual or ethical constraints. In true Promethean fashion, these experiments force us to confront, expand, and adapt our view of what it means to be human.

In the contemporary era, Prometheus offers an updated perspective on those aspects of the human condition that his myth has addressed so effectively over the ages. Contemporary artists and writers continue to find all aspects of his story compelling – the theft of fire, his subsequent punishment and liberation, his creation of humans. We will see that, just as in the Romantic period, he symbolizes the triumphant and transcendent spirit of the artist. In addition, while Prometheus has been associated with the human need to work since Hesiod's time, the incredible transformation of the workplace over the course of the nineteenth and twentieth centuries has also attracted writers and thinkers to Prometheus with even more intensity. From the industrial revolution to the digital revolution, the needs and concerns of workers have been at odds with those of management, and Prometheus' willingness to stand up to the boss has inspired resistance to harsh and unfair working conditions to this day. With even greater influence, Prometheus has been called upon to think about our love affair with technology, and as before, the tensions built into his story have inspired some serious soul searching about the promises and dangers of unchecked technological innovation. These three themes – the role of the artist, the conditions of work, and the consequences of technology – are at the heart of Tony Harrison's *Prometheus*, and a closer look at this film will give us a better understanding of what the twentieth century has made of the god who stole fire.

TONY HARRISON'S *PROMETHEUS*

Prometheus, Tony Harrison's first feature film, makes the Titan's rebellious theft of fire the setting for his rather bleak look at how things stand in Britain at the end of the twentieth century – politically and economically. Tony Harrison was born in Leeds in 1937 and has published several volumes of poetry and works for the theatre, for which he is celebrated as one of Britain's leading theatre and film poets. Harrison has translated several Greek dramas for the contemporary stage, and his work represents a brilliant and often provocative fusion of the ancient and contemporary worlds. As a poet, Harrison produces urgent contemporary responses to public events even as he is deeply indebted to the classical tradition. Like the Greeks and Romantics before him, Harrison reworks Prometheus' myth in the context of his own time and culture.

In the 1970s and 1980s, Britain's Conservative governments led by Edward Heath (1970–74) and Margaret Thatcher (1979–90) and the

National Union of Mineworkers were engaged in a set of high-stakes political struggles resulting in the most violent and destructive strikes in modern British history. It is in this recent historical context that Harrison revisits and reworks the themes of technological progress and political rebellion that were first dramatized in fifth-century Athens by Aeschylus' *Prometheus Bound*.

Although the film is not a strict translation or even an adaptation – one critic called it an imitation – of Aeschylus' play, it takes the classical Greek play as a clear point of departure (the main character's grandson even recites lines from the Aeschylean play at the film's beginning). All of Aeschylus' characters are present although radically adapted and updated: Kratos and Bia are menacing power workers, complete with black chemical exposure masks; the Oceanids have become women workers from a fish factory. Mam, the mother of a young boy from the mining community turns into Io, ranging across Eastern Europe and taking on the black and white appearance of a Friesian cow due to her exposure to chemicals and carbon. Drawing upon the contemporary fears about mad cow disease, her death is gruesomely represented as the senseless slaughter of a cow (Harrison used the mad cow abattoir at Stockport for the scene), bringing together the inhumane treatment of animals and the desecration of the environment. Hermes appears dressed in a silver jumpsuit that, as one critic put it, parodies 'the high-tech mufti worn in those spotless post-Fordist plants in which new work has taken root since Thatcher's cull'. Hermes' upper-middle-class accent underscores his adversarial relationship with the Prometheus figure of the film – a cancer-ridden, former Yorkshire coal miner, and their dialogue forms the backbone of the film.

Harrison's Prometheus opens with a shot of steaming cooling towers and soon shifts to the interior of a house near the Kirkby Main colliery, with a shot of a newspaper with a headline announcing the closing of the last coal mine in Yorkshire. While his father grimly gets ready for his last day of work in the coal mine, a young boy doggedly tries to memorize lines from Aeschylus' *Prometheus Bound* for his homework. He tries to summarize the myth for his father, explaining that Prometheus was chained to a rock for thirty thousand years with an eagle eating his liver every day as punishment for his theft of fire, 'so now/ there's coal and all that'. To which his father replies:

> Serves him bloody reet for thieving. And he shouldn't have
> Bloody bothered, if pits was his idea!
>
> (9)

In particular what Harrison takes from Aeschylus' drama is its political orientation – his is a rebellious Prometheus, too – and its emphasis on the prospect of suffering on a millennial scale. As the playwright says in his introductory essay to the screenplay of the film, 'Fire and Poetry',

> No play in the ancient repertoire works over a longer time scale than *Prometheus Bound*. Or deals with more unbroken suffering. Its span is not, as in the *Oresteia*, the ten fateful years of the Trojan War, but thirty millenia: thirty millennia of tyrannical torture, thirty millennia of defiance.
>
> (viii)

Harrison's use of Aeschylus is mediated, however, through Percy Shelley's *Prometheus Unbound*, a connection that Harrison, himself, makes in his preface. He tells us that he wrote this introductory essay in the Baths of Caracalla in Rome, the very site where Shelley wrote his own *Prometheus Unbound*. In particular, Harrison responds to Shelley's refusal to let his Prometheus reconcile with Zeus' authoritarian regime, and Harrison's essay helps articulate the significant role that Shelley's poem has played in the appropriation of Prometheus' myth by the socialist cause. Harrison recalls Karl Marx's alleged lament over Shelley's early death: 'for Shelley was a thorough revolutionary and would have remained in the van of socialism all his life' (xv). Within this revolutionary context Harrison observes that 'the myth of Prometheus who brought fire to mankind keeps entering history at significant moments' (vii). The monumental time-scale of the myth, encompassing 30,000 years and many generations of humankind, allows for a continual reassessment of the human condition at times of oppression and suffering. So, like Shelley at the beginning of the nineteenth century, Harrison at the end of the twentieth calls upon Prometheus to help him (and us) think about technology and revolution, art and work, and their place in the contemporary human experience.

The action of the film takes the implications of Prometheus' thieving further than the British coal industry, however. The ageing miner spends much of the film in the dilapidated Palace Cinema in Knottingley, where he watches the journey of a monumental gilded statue of Prometheus (forged from melted-down miners) transported across post-industrial Europe to be ritually destroyed by fire at Eleusis, the birthplace of Aeschylus. Throughout the film, the hero – a chain-smoking socialist – engages in a dialogue with Hermes, Zeus' representative, and refuses to capitulate to the rule of gods, cancer, or capitalists. Harrison thus extends the scope of his film beyond working-class England to include the bombings at Dresden, the Holocaust, and the industrially ravaged landscapes of eastern Europe – all products of Promethean technology and victims of the endless iterations of Zeus' authoritarian regime.

THE TECHNOLOGICAL PROMETHEUS

From the wheezing coal miner to the ominously masked Kratos and Bia, from the devastating force exhibited in the bombing of Dresden to the catastrophic environmental wasteland of a post-industrial eastern Europe, Harrison's *Prometheus* exposes the risks and destructive potential of technology. At one point in the film, Hermes sits with a drink in the Bar Meksyk in Poland and comments on the smoking chimneys from the industrial complex of Nowa Huta:

> So such Promethean shrines,
> chemical and steel works, mines,
> still anger Zeus because they stand
> for the Promethean contraband,
> Nonetheless make him content
> by blighting Man's environment.
>
> (63)

Originally built as part of what Harrison calls 'the pattern of rapid Promethean industrialisation', the steel works at Nowa Huta have stood abandoned since 1989, symbols of the collapse of industrialization in Eastern Europe. Earlier, Hermes elaborates Zeus' glee over the devastating effects of pollution on humankind:

> children coughing, little tots
> with nebulizers in their cots,
> cancer and asthma . . .
>
> (62)

Hermes notes that whereas Prometheus' technology was once 'flaunted', in the end the hope and promise of industrialization have had unanticipated and devastating effects for humankind. Cancer and asthma, illnesses unheard of in Hesiod's time, appear here as dramatic and deadly escalations of those much more vague and general diseases that escaped from Pandora's jar to bring trouble to mortals in archaic Greece.

Harrison's *Prometheus* symbolizes not just the unforeseen consequences of man's development of technology – illness, damage to the environment – but also the deliberately deadly uses of fire, especially in the context of war. As the cattle truck bearing Prometheus' statue prepares to enter Dresden, the city devastated by air attacks in World War II, Hermes observes:

> And Dresden, city of destructive flame,
> 's the best for blackening his good name.
> Those 35,000 fire flayed
> won't cheer Prometheus on parade.
> Nor will their descendants cheer
> when we take Prometheus here.
>
> (41)

Dresden, like fifth-century Athens, a city celebrated for its artistic and cultural treasures, was reduced to rubble by the ravages of war, Athens by fire and Dresden by wartime bombing. In chapter 2, we saw how fifth-century Athenians in the wake of their own destruction by the Persians looked to Prometheus – through cult and on stage – to make sense of the devastating potential of fire.

In another play adapted from an ancient Greek source, *The Labourers of Herakles*, Harrison himself alludes to this Athenian experience. In a speech delivered by Heracles atop his own funeral pyre, the hero elaborates this theme of the power of fire:

> The Greek shrines gutted by Persians, after Plataea,
> had their holy fires rekindled with the Delphic flame from here.
> The fire that burned Miletos and the flame
> that makes me writhe with anguish are the very same
> element that we hold up here tonight
> as a beacon for the future with its ambiguous light.
>
> (*The Labourers of Herakles*: 123)

In the *Prometheus*, Harrison updates this theme of fire first with respect to the damage to the environment sustained as a result of technological progress. Next he shines its 'ambiguous light' on the atrocities of world wars, especially the Holocaust of the twentieth century, which, Hermes explains, 'Zeus approved . . . and endorsed' (59). Through ritual torch-races and the staging of Prometheus as fire-giver, the Athenians attempted to reclaim the productive and celebratory power of fire after the devastation they suffered at the hands of the Persian army. Evoking these fifth-century Athenian rituals of fire, Harrison exploits the use of fire as both a tool of annihilation and a means of commemoration in a scene set near Auschwitz, Poland, the city whose name has become synonymous with the horrors of Nazi death camps. The trailer truck that has carried the statue of Prometheus across eastern Europe is filled with candles of the sort lit by Jewish pilgrims in commemoration of those killed in the Holocaust, and Hermes, again speaking as Zeus' mouthpiece, condemns the use of these candles, 'stolen fire in little spikes':

> Why? Why is it fire that they choose?
> These candles that can help them cope
> with history and lack of hope
> are anathema to Fuhrer Zeus
> who hates fire's sacramental use,

Jews flaunting in Lord Zeus's face
The fire he'd meant to end their race.

(61)

Again, it comes back to the fundamental duality of fire as a source of both destruction and commemoration, and the Holocaust stands, as so often, for the most extreme expression of that power.

And so, Tony Harrison's *Prometheus* offers a searing critique of the uses to which technology has been put in the twentieth century. Its original benefits, whatever they were, have been long since overshadowed by its destructive powers. In the following speech of Hermes, Harrison spins out the negative repercussions of Prometheus' gift of fire from a smoker's cough to the coal miner's black lung. Hermes explains that Zeus is pleased that Prometheus' gift has turned out so badly for humankind. Zeus no longer has to plan to eradicate the human race since men are doing such a good job on their own with smog, pollution, cancer – all by-products of Prometheus' gift:

So Armageddon's put on hold
till Zeus is bored or Man too bold.

(31)

Tony Harrison's *Prometheus* combines Aeschylus' celebration of the technological potential represented by Prometheus' theft of fire for mankind with Hesiod's sense of human despair and powerlessness in the face of the gods. Hesiod's Prometheus sketches out a picture of the human experience that is defined by back-breaking hard work, sickness, and a meagre existence, especially when compared to the Golden Age of the Homeric poems. For Aeschylus, the myth of Prometheus describes the very different experience of early fifth-century Athens, and his Prometheus celebrates the skills and accomplishments, technological and otherwise, that Prometheus' gift of fire set in motion for humankind.

While Harrison echoes Aeschylus' focus on the potential of technology to ameliorate the human condition, he tempers this optimism with a Hesiodic dose of realism. In the end, technology has brought nothing but sickness, war, and back-breaking work. As Harrison notes,

But if Aeschylus had lived today
he'd have to write a different play.
He'd change his verses once he'd seen a
burn-off flame at Elefsina,
the chimneys pouring smoke above
the ancient site he used to love . . .

(81)

Aeschylus' vision needs to be revised in light of recent events, and Tony Harrison's twentieth-century *Prometheus* narrates a decline in the human condition that can be directly traced to abuses of the technology that emerged from the Titan's gift of fire. His cold, hard, spin-doctoring Hermes is the product of a grim world-view in which humans have been once again tricked by the gods, helpless victims of their games and power plays.

While some technological innovations in the workplace, in medicine, or in the means of communication have greatly enhanced the human experience in the twentieth century, the unintended consequences of others have brought destruction to the human race on an unparalleled scale and threaten still more. Tony Harrison's *Prometheus* revises Prometheus' role as patron saint of technology to help us ask difficult questions about its role in our lives. What are the ethical and social implications of technological advances? What are the human costs of progress? Harrison's answers to the questions invoked by the Prometheus myth are very grim.

PROMETHEUS AND THE WORKER: *HOMO FABER*

Harrison's focus on the use and abuse of technology leads him inevitably to the role of work in the twentieth century, and *Prometheus* brings together technology and rebellion in ways that explore the role of the worker, *homo faber*, within a technological world as well. Associated with both the ideal of labour and revolutions against the abuse of power, Harrison's Prometheus symbolizes not just technological prowess, but also the possibilities of work, social justice, and workers' rights.

Harrison brings the figure of Prometheus, famous for representing the downtrodden and oppressed in a dialectical struggle with authoritarian regimes, to focus on the working man, particularly within the context of industrialization. Known for making humans out of clay, and worshipped in Athens by potters, Prometheus has always been associated with the human need and capacity for work. In archaic Greece, we remember, his myth is linked specifically with agriculture and with a view of the human experience defined primarily by the constant need to work the land. The context for work may change over time, from ploughing fields to assembling cars to coal mining or data processing, but the human need to work does not, and that is an essential part of the Promethean myth.

In his introductory essay, Harrison points out that, due in part to the revolutionary poetry of Shelley and Byron, Prometheus gradually came to be associated with the socialist cause. In *Prometheus and the Bolsheviks*, a 1937 book on the Caucasus (the fateful mountain venue on the contemporary border between the Russian federation, Georgia, and Azerbaijan where Prometheus was chained to the rock), the English poet and magazine editor, John Lehman, invoked Prometheus as a powerful symbol of the Bolshevik cause to deliver man from tyranny and barbarism by seizing material power. In the book's final chapter, Lehman recounts a dream of Prometheus that he had while sleeping aboard a Soviet steamer crossing the Black Sea. In this dream the Titan says to him: 'I find myself passionately on the side of the Bolsheviks when I hear accounts of the Civil War struggles. It reminds me of my own struggles with Jove over the fire business' (Lehman 1937: 254). Prometheus then announces that he has decided to join the Party.

Of course, the association between Prometheus and the cause of socialism has a venerable provenance. Karl Marx himself referred to Prometheus in his early work as 'the first saint and martyr of the philosopher's calendar'. During his editorship of the *Rhineland Gazette*, Karl Marx was depicted in cartoons as Prometheus bound to a printing press with the Prussian eagle gnawing his liver. At his feet, an Aeschylean chorus of Oceanids represented the cities of the Rhineland pleading for freedom (Fig. 13). The Marxist theorist Leszek Kolakowski articulates the Promethean element of Marx's work explaining that 'Marx was certain that the proletariat as the collective

Figure 13 Karl Marx as Prometheus, allegory on the prohibition of the *Rheinische Zeitung*.

Source: Photo from Karl Marx. Frederick Engels, Collected Works, vol. 1, New York: International Publishers, (1975), 374–75

Prometheus would, in the universal revolution, sweep away the age-long contradiction between the interest of the individual and that of the species' (Kolakowski 1978: 1. 412–13).

The classicist George Thomson calls Aeschylus' Prometheus 'the patron saint of the proletariat', and it is in this tradition of the collective experience of work that Tony Harrison sets his Promethean film amidst the collapse of the mining industry in the north of England. One of the first scenes from the film focuses on pages from Yorkshire papers announcing recent pit closures. The miner has been saving these papers, a scrapbook of sorts documenting the miners' strike going 'reet back to '84', but his son has thrown them on the fire to which he exclaims, 'It's bad enough being jobless wi'out being chucked on t'fire by thee!' (10). The scene clearly reinterprets the Aeschylean Prometheus (illustrated in the boy's textbook as a golden statue with his right fist raised in defiance and brandishing a flaming rod of fennel stalk in his left) as the striking miner, represented by the grandfather's coal carving of a miner in pit gear in the same pose. An etched brass caption reads 'Striking Miner, 1984'. Whereas Shelley's Prometheus focuses on authoritarian political regimes and the tyranny of the monarchies ruling Europe at the end of the eighteenth century, Harrison relocates Prometheus' rebellion to the workplace. He rewrites the political struggle of peasant versus king as that of worker versus management.

Over the course of the movie this powerful symbol of striking coal miners blurs easily into other scenes and traces of working-class rebellion, the most provocative of which is smoking. In an interview, Harrison explains his use of smoking in the film in part as a very specific way of translating Greek mythology into a contemporary vernacular:

> So the cigarette becomes the fennel stalk, an emblem of what man has done with fire. It is destructive, but they don't give it up. It also becomes the idea of fire being forbidden to man and used to destroy man. This kind of constant forbidding of things is just another version of that. In this case it is all about smoking.

Smoking also functions here as a kind of self-destructive sign of the working class and its total commitment to resistance. Hermes, playing the role of Zeus' henchman, takes the opportunity in the film to represent Zeus' authoritarian regime in all its manifestations, including enforcing the 'no-smoking law' in the derelict movie theatre where the old man sits chain-smoking and reminiscing about the good old days when everyone smoked, both on and off screen. The old man rises from his seat into the pose of Prometheus, shaking his fist in defiance of the image of Hermes on the screen and cries out, 'Smokers of the world unite!' (30).

Cigarettes, Harrison's reworking of Hesiod's fennel stalk, represent the working man's last gesture of resistance against authoritarian regimes in all their guises – political, economic, and medical – and become the ironic symbol of the failure of resistance in all its forms. The working man is dying from 'coal-face work or cigarettes', and Hermes, with his posh accent and his elegant silver boots represents the dominant power structure, victorious once again. The old man taunts Hermes, blowing smoke (both figuratively and literally) and boasting: 'And I were glad we could produce/fuel for fires that angered Zeus' (55). But as the old man collapses into his seat with the efforts of his defiance, Hermes smugly replies that all that time spent 'groveling underground in grime' was wasted, destined to come to ''Nowt! Nowt! Nowt! Nowt!':

> History spat you out like phlegm,
> shop-steward of the NUM
> expecting, of all things, to create
> in class-torn Britain a fair state!
> So I'd unclench your weedy fist
> you smoke-demolished Socialist.
> (56)

So much for Shelley's vision of a state 'sceptreless, free, uncircumscribed'. While Harrison embraces Shelley's refusal to let oppressor and oppressed reconcile, he rejects the Romantic poet's utopian vision of a classless state as well. In this respect, Harrison's Prometheus is more like that of Byron, caught in a perpetual state of defiance.

The implosion of Prometheus' support of the working man is crystallized in a night-time scene in a foundry when a cattle truck full of miners tips them into a fiery cauldron, thus recycling them into the golden figure of Prometheus himself. In this respect, Harrison revisits an aspect of the Promethean myth that was already present in Hesiod – namely the difficulty, the sheer futility, of man's working existence as a result of Prometheus. Without the intervention of Prometheus, Hesiod laments that 'You might get enough done in one day/To keep you fixed for a year without working' (*Works and Days*: 43–44). But ever since Prometheus tricked Zeus, the king of gods has made life hard for humans. While in both Hesiod and Harrison's world-views, it is work that defines human existence vis à vis the gods, new in the twentieth-century reprise of this theme is the notion of the collective identity of workers versus authoritarian figures in the guise of management. Again, Harrison has brought the political focus of Aeschylus and Shelley together with Hesiod's lament about man's need to work in a new way.

FIRE AND POETRY

In addition to his association with technology and the experience of work, Prometheus continues to symbolize the artist's creativity in the twentieth century. Whereas the Romantic poets Goethe and Byron compare their own poetic act of creation with Prometheus' creation of humankind, each fashioning himself as a 'new Prometheus', Harrison equates poetic creativity with fire itself. He opens his essay on 'Fire and Poetry' with the following memory:

> As a child I learned to dream awake before the coal-fire in our living room. Staring into the fire, with its ever-changing flames, shifting coals, falling ash, and what were called 'strangers' – skins of soot flapping on the grate – evoked in me my first poetry. . . . I have always associated staring into flames with the freedom of poetic meditation.
>
> (vii)

The mysterious and dynamic power of the flames sparks the creative process – yet another way in which humankind has evolved beyond its primal state. As the Promethean old man says near the end of the film:

> Fire, that's brought Man close t' brink
> were t'first to help him dream and think.
> Imagine men first freed from t'night
> first sitting round t'warm firelight,
> safe from t'beasts they allus feared
> until Prometheus first appeared.
>
> (83)

Harrison's meditation on the inspirational power of fire here does more than locate the artistic process in the glowing embers of a fire. It also suggests that we revisit those passages of Aeschylus' *Prometheus Bound* and even Mary Shelley's *Frankenstein* that articulated man's state of progress from a grim bestial existence through the discovery of fire to the conquest of nature and a more physically comfortable and intellectual life. Prometheus' theft of fire led, inevitably, not just to technological innovation but also to social innovation – the creation of institutions such as sacrifice and skills such as medicine, and, finally, to poetry or what Aeschylus calls 'the combination of letters as a means of remembering all things, mother of the muses, skilled worker'. Fire, as Harrison suggests, is key to both man's physical comfort and his intellectual accomplishments. Free from the cold and fear, we are able to be creative; Prometheus' technological gift is thus intimately connected to his artistic one.

Towards the end of his introductory essay, Harrison comments on his decision to tell Prometheus' story as a movie: 'The connection between my obsession with fire and my obsession with movies led me to make a film about fire and poetry' (xxii). He explains that the technology of cinema has the power to give heroic stature to a humble face, thus transforming the figures on screen into gods, a power emblematic of the Promethean spirit. Harrison thus extends his childhood experience of gazing into the fire into that of making movies to be watched within a darkened theatre – it is all about the power of light to reveal reality out of the darkness, to create art out of the everyday experience of men and women. As the chain-smoking, coal-mining Promethean figure from Harrison's movie puts it: 'Fire and poetry, two great powers/that mek the so-called gods' world OURS!' (84)

For in Harrison's *Prometheus*, poetry, like fire, has its origins in the divine realm. As Hermes explains early in the film, poetry is the language of the gods: 'It's quite beyond mere mortal reach,/this pure Olympian form of speech' (21). In this respect, all poets are Promethean figures, stealing the poetic spark that marks the diction of the divine world, and using it to bring light to human affairs. As Hermes complains:

Constant theft! First, fire, now this –
pinching poetic artifice!
How can Olympus stay intact
if *poetry* comes to *Pontefract*?

(23)

Both fire and poetry have been stolen from the gods, not given, and Harrison characterizes their presence in the world of humans as parallel acts of rebellion against the gods. As Hermes complains:

Poets have taught Mankind to breach
the boundaries Zeus put round speech,
and the fire Prometheus stole
created man's poetic soul.

(44)

The theft of poetic speech is thus just one more iteration of Prometheus' transgression upon the divine world on behalf of humankind. And in this respect, Harrison, like Shelley and the other Romantic poets before him, fuses the aesthetic and the political dimensions of Prometheus' myth. Through the creative power of the poetic imagination, mere mortals can remake their own world; as Shelley said, 'poets are the unacknowledged legislators of the world'. Harrison inverts the idealism of Shelley's belief in the Promethean power of the poet, however, by comparing it to fire and by emphasizing its purloined status. Like fire, poetry was stolen from Zeus, and as a result humankind will pay a harsh penalty for it. Whereas the Romantic vision (with the exception of Mary Shelley's *Frankenstein*) is one of poets helping imagine a better world for humankind, Harrison's view is bleaker – he underscores the power of poetry by elaborating just how angry the gods are at losing their exclusive use of it.

And yet, Harrison's vision is not entirely without hope, for it is through poetry, this rebellious act of creation, that humankind can craft a response – perhaps the only response in the end – to the suffering that marks the human condition. Harrison's movie conjures up a fairly bleak view of the long-term effects of Prometheus' theft of fire for humankind. Far from Aeschylus' world of endless possibility, his (and ours) is a world constrained by the devastating potential of technology – pollution, holocaust, war – and the endless challenges of the workplace. And yet, Harrison tells us, Prometheus has given us a very powerful tool that can help us cope with this dismal state of affairs as well. In an interview, Harrison said that poetry ' should address the hardest things in life, and the most powerful weapon it brings to the fray is its own form'. In his preface he reminds us that from the time of Greek tragedy on, poetry and other forms of art give us a way to cope with the limitations and challenges of the human condition.

ETYMOLOGIES: WHAT USE IS PROMETHEUS?

At the beginning of his movie, Tony Harrison plays with the etymology of Prometheus' name. Hesiod, we remember, highlighted the trickery (*metis*) at the heart of Prometheus' name in his *Theogony*, and Aeschylus exploited the irony inherent in his reading of the god's name at the beginning of the *Prometheus Bound*. As Might prepares to leave Prometheus alone, bound to the mountain crag, he taunts him:

> The Gods named you Forethought falsely, for you yourself need forethought to find a way to escape from this device.
>
> (*Prometheus Bound*: 86–87)

Harrison takes up this etymological tradition with a contemporary twist. At the beginning of his film Harrison has the central character question his son about Prometheus:

Dad: So who's Pro-me-the-us when he's at home.
Boy: It's pronounced Pro-me-theus.
       PROM-ME-THEUS . . . USE . . . USE
Dad: So what bloody *use* wor'e then?

(9)

This unemployed Yorkshire coal miner may have his reservations about what an ancient Greek god can do for him, but, as Harrison shows us, it is the mythic power of the god who stole fire to help humankind that helps him tell the story of twentieth-century working-class England. As we have seen in the preceding chapters, Prometheus' myth – even his name – turns out to be particularly 'useful' as different cultures at different times adapt, revise, and renew the story of the god who stole fire for humankind.

OVERVIEW

In the twentieth century, Prometheus in all his mythic complexity inspired us to redefine the parameters of the human condition in light of a century of incomparable achievements in politics, science, and the arts as well as unparalleled destruction on a massive scale. The Prometheus who stole fire for mankind helped poets and scientists alike explore the benefits and risks of technology. How do new medical technologies affect our definitions of human life? How have innovations in the means of production affected the way we work and the way we think of ourselves as workers? The Prometheus who dared oppose an authoritarian Zeus to save mankind has guided politicians and playwrights in their attempts to evaluate the limitations of being mortal and the ways that art or governmental structures can help transcend them.

From its vantage point at the end of the twentieth century, Tony Harrison's 1998 movie *Prometheus* offers a devastating critique of the uses to which the Titans' gift of fire have been put in that doleful century of war, division, and untold disappointments for all who hoped for the liberation of mankind. The Holocaust, environmental degradation, and class warfare are all part of Zeus' plan to punish mortals for Prometheus' intervention in mortal affairs. And yet the spirits of rebellion and of creativity that define the human condition continue to thrive in spite of it all, and Harrison's Prometheus, like that of Byron, celebrates the power of the human imagination as the ultimate source of resistance. Harrison's film looks back to the mythic tradition of both Hesiod and Aeschylus through the lens of Shelley's *Prometheus Unbound*. While Harrison's movie reprises the perennial Promethean themes of rebellion, imagination, and suffering in a uniquely twentieth-century context, it also serves as the ideal text from which to draw some conclusions about Prometheus' broader mythic significance.

In looking back at Prometheus in these very different historical and cultural settings, we must agree with Tony Harrison's observation that the myth of Prometheus enters our consciousness at significant moments of history – at times of great prosperity and of scarce resources, at moments of technological triumph and of catastrophic disaster. As a model of human ingenuity and a symbol of mortal suffering, he personifies the best and the worst of the human condition. And yet, while Prometheus has been invoked by Greek and Romantic poets, by scientists, musicians, and political theorists alike, his myth offers no clear answers to the challenging questions that plague us. What is the nature of power? What is the place of humans in the larger cosmic scheme of things? Can we transcend the suffering of our world through art? Can we overcome the limitations of our world through technology? What is the human cost of progress? Prometheus' myth does not hold the answers to any of these questions. In fact, it pointedly refuses to define the human experience universally nor does it celebrate it unconditionally. Instead, Prometheus' myth will always help us pose the key questions that face each new age about what it means to be human. And in this respect, as Tony Harrison suggests, he'll always be bloody useful!

FURTHER READING

INTRODUCING PROMETHEUS

The primary classical sources for the myth of Prometheus are Hesiod, *Works and Days* 41–105; *Theogony* 507–616; Aeschylus, *Prometheus Bound*; Apollodorus, *Library* 1.2.2ff.; 1.3.6; 1.7.1–2; 2.5.4; 2.5.11 3.13.5; Pausanias, *Description of Greece* 1.30.2; 2.19.5; 2.19.8; Hyginus, *Fabulae* 54, 142, 144; *Poetica astronomica* 2.6; 2.15; 2.42. A good translation of Aesop's fables is Gibbs (trans.) (2002) *Aesop's Fables*. For discussions of the etymology of Prometheus' name, see Martin West's footnote on *Theogony* 510 together with note 3 in Watkins (1995), p. 256.

For a thorough list of literary references and visual representations of Prometheus in classical antiquity, see the entry on Prometheus in the *Lexicon Iconographicum Mythologicae Graecae*. For a list that covers the period from 1300 to the 1990s, see the entry on Prometheus in Reid (1993). Prometheus has been the subject of several books and articles tracing a historical narrative of his appearance in works of art and literature over the ages. See, for example, Séchan (1951); Trousson (1976) and Raggio (1958). Carl Kerényi's (1963) book, *Prometheus. Archetypal Image of Human Existence*, offers an analytical treatment of the myth in Jungian terms. Donoghue (1974) addresses aspects of the Prometheus myth in a series of essays on American literature.

For more on Clifford Geertz's notion of 'thinking with' the symbolic elements of another culture, see his introductory essay, 'Thick Description: Toward an Interpretive Theory of Culture' (1973). Roland Barthes' essay, 'Myth Today,' at the end of *Mythologies* (1957), offers a structural analysis of myth as a system of communication that continues to be useful. Other treatments of the notion of myth in general or of Greek myth more specifically include the introduction to Martin (2003); Detienne (1986); Buxton (1994); and Lincoln (1999).

I THE TRICKSTER

All the translations from Hesiod here are from Stanley Lombardo's (1993) translation of *Hesiod's Works and Days and Theogony*. These translations are accompanied by a very helpful introduction by Robert Lamberton; see also Lamberton (1988). For texts and detailed commentary on these poems (as well as on related topics), see the editions of Martin West: *Hesiod, Theogony* (1966) and *Hesiod, Works and Days* (1978). For a general introduction to Hesiod, see Nagy (1990), especially for the discussion of the etymology of Hesiod's name. For discussion of poetic persona and voice, see Griffith (1983a) and Martin (1992). For the historical background of the poems, see Finley (1970) and Snodgrass (1980). See also Tandy and Neale (1996).

Jean-Pierre Vernant has made the most significant contributions to the study of the myth of Prometheus in Hesiod, and my discussion here owes a great deal to his work. See Vernant (1980) and Vernant (1986).

On the role of Pandora in the Prometheus myth and related gender issues, see Zeitlin (1996); Arthur (1982), and Sussman (1978). On the evolution of the Pandora myth after Hesiod, see Panofsky and Panofsky (1956).

For comparative studies of the trickster figure, see Pelton (1980); Ricketts (1965); Radin (1956); the essays collected in Hynes and Doty (1993) and those in Janik (1998). For a discussion of the trickster in Greek mythology, see Brown (1947); and Kerényi (1956). For discussions of the theme of trickery or cunning in Greek literature, see Detienne and Vernant (1974).

2 THE CULT OF PROMETHEUS AT ATHENS

For studies on the role and significance of fire in Greek religion, see Burkert (1985) and Furley (1981). For an entertaining and informative collection of myths and legends surrounding the discovery and invention of fire, see Frazer (1930).

For the topography and archaeology of Athens, see Camp (2001) and Travlos (1971). On the buildings and destruction of Athens, see Camp (2001); Thompson (1981); Shear (1993).

On the cult of Prometheus and the Prometheia, see Deubner (1932). The evidence for the torch race in general and especially Prometheus' connection to it is scarce, and often evidence from the torch race at one festival, especially the Panathenaea, is used to explain all torch races. For the torch race as an athletic event in Athens, see Kyle (1987); for the ritual significance of the torch race, especially with respect to the Panathenaea, see Robertson (1985). For a collection of all the evidence for the torch race in Athens, see Sterett (1901).

For representations of Prometheus on vase paintings in the company of satyrs, see Beazely (1939); Webster (1972). On representations of satyrs more generally both on stage and on vases, see Lissarrague (1990); and Berard (1989). For a general discussion of the genre of the satyr play, see Sutton (1980) and Griffith (2002). For the fragments of the *Prometheus Fire-Kindler*, see the third volume of *Tragicorum graecorum fragmenta*, edited by Stefan Radt (1985). Carl Kerényi (1963) collects and translates the fragments of the satyr play, *Prometheus Fire-Kindler* in his *Prometheus*, 69–72.

3 POLITICAL REBEL AND CULTURAL HERO

For the Greek text and commentary of Aeschylus' *Prometheus Bound*, see Griffith (1983b). For a good, clear translation of the *Prometheus Bound*, see David Grene's (1956) translation. For discussions of the authenticity question, see Griffith (1977); Herington (1970); and the more recent Lloyd-Jones (2003). For general literary studies of the play, see Conacher (1980); Thomson (1972); and Saïd (1985).

On the issue of progress in the classical Greek world, see the following useful discussions: Dodds (1973); Edelstein (1967); and Guthrie (1957).

For a translation of Plato's *Protagoras*, see Guthrie (1956); for a commentary on the dialogue, see Coby (1987). For discussions of the myth of Prometheus in this dialogue, see Miller (1978); and Ferrain (2000).

For the Greek text and commentary on Aristophanes' *Birds*, see Dunbar's (1995) edition and Sommerstein (1987), who includes a translation facing the text. For a discussion of the *Birds* and the Prometheus trilogy, see Herington (1963).

4 THE ROMANTIC PROMETHEUS

Quotations from the various poets and authors discussed in this chapter come from the following editions: McGann (1986), Zillman (1968); Middleton (1983); and Butler (1993), whose edition has a very helpful introduction to the novel as well as several appendices that outline and reprint the changes made to the 1831 revision. Also included is Mary Shelley's introduction to the later revision. Although the 1831 version was long the preferred text, I have followed Marilyn Butler (and others) in my decision to use the original 1818 version here, preferring its unrevised reflection on important social and moral issues attending creativity, scientific exploration, and the limits of the human condition.

Prometheus, of course, continued to be popular between the classical Greek period and Romanticism. For a review of the myth of Prometheus from antiquity to the eighteenth century, see Raggio (1958). On the relationship between Milton and the Romantics, see Trott (1998). For more general introductions to the mythic figure of Prometheus in the Romantic period, see Trousson (2001); Raizis (1983); and Bush (1937). Hans Blumenberg's (1985) book *Work on Myth* includes a provocative discussion of Prometheus within the broader topic of European intellectual thought. Also helpful for general background on the Romantic movement are Wu (1998) and Curran (1993).

On the Political Prometheus, see Lewis (1992); and Curran (1986). On Prometheus and Napoleon, see Bloom (1971a); and Bainbridge (1995).

See also the following books and articles on more specific topics. On Shelley's *Prometheus Unbound*, see chapter 3 of Cantor (1984); Wasserman (1971); Bennett and Curran (1996); and Bloom (1971b). For a comparison of the role of Prometheus as it appears in the works of Byron and Shelley, see Robinson (1976); and Raizis (1983). For a biographical and historical introduction to Goethe, see the extremely useful essays in the *Cambridge Companion to Goethe*, ed. Sharpe (2002). On Mary Shelley's *Frankenstein*, see the informative chapter, 'The Nightmare of Romantic Idealism' (especially its title), of Paul A. Cantor's (1984) book. See also Small (1972).

5 PROMETHEUS IN THE CONTEMPORARY AGE

For an annotated list of works of artists, writers, and poets dealing with the myth of Prometheus, see Reid (1993). For a review of theatrical works devoted to Prometheus, see Lorna Hardwick's essay on Tony Harrison (2000). For more on José Clemente Orozco's Prometheus mural, see the collection of essays, edited by Marjorie L. Harth (2001). For those who draw upon Prometheus in discussions of technology, see Barney (2000); De Ropp (1972); and Mitzman (2003). On the adoption of Prometheus as symbol of socialism and the working class, see Leszek Kolakowski (1978). See also Tony Harrison's thoughtful introductory essay 'Fire and Poetry,' where I encountered many useful references, such as Lehman (1937).

Tony Harrison's *Prometheus*, a Channel 4 film, was produced in association with the Arts Council of England. The screenplay was published by Faber and Faber (1998) with an introductory essay, 'Fire and Poetry'. For critical discussions of Harrison's *Prometheus*, see Hall (2002); Hardwick's (2000) essay on Harrison's *Prometheus*, and the essays by Hardwick, Robinson, and Woodward published from the Department of Classical Studies, The Open University, Open Colloquium 1999, 'Tony Harrison's Poetry Drama and Film: The Classical Dimension' (http://www.open.ac.uk/Arts/Colq99/). For more general studies of Harrison, see Kelleher (1996); and Byrne (1997).

WORKS CITED

Ackerman, H.C. and J.-R. Gisler (eds) (1981–99) *Lexicon iconographicum mythologiae classicae*, Zurich: Artemis.

Arthur, M. (1982) 'Cultural Strategies in Hesiod's *Theogony*: Law, Family, and Society', *Arethusa* 15: 63–82.

Bainbridge, S. (1995) *Napoleon and English Romanticism*, Cambridge: Cambridge University Press.

Barney, D. (2000) *Prometheus Wired: The Hope for Democracy in the Age of Network Technology*, Chicago: University of Chicago Press.

Barthes, R. [1957] (1972) *Mythologies*, trans. A. Lavers, New York: The Noonday Press.

Beazely, J.D. (1939) 'Prometheus Fire-Lighter,' *American Journal of Archaeology* 43: 618–39.

Bennett, B. and S. Curran (eds) (1996) *Shelley: Poet and Legislator of the World*, Baltimore/London: Johns Hopkins University Press.

Berard, C. (1989) *A City of Images*, trans. D. Lyons, Princeton: Princeton University Press.

Bloom, H. (1971a) 'Napoleon and Prometheus: The Romantic Myth of Organic Energy', in *Ringers in the Tower*, Chicago: University of Chicago Press, 81–84.

—— (1971b) 'The Unpastured Sea: An Introduction to Shelley', in *Ringers in the Tower*, Chicago: University of Chicago Press, 87–116.

Blumenberg, H. (1985) *Work on Myth*, trans. R. Wallace, Cambridge, MA: MIT Press.

Brown, N.O. (1947) *Hermes the Thief*, Madison, WI: University of Wisconsin Press.

Burkert, W. (1985) 'Fire Rituals', in *Greek Religion*, trans. J. Raffan, Cambridge, MA: Harvard University Press, 60–64.

Bush, D. (1937) *Mythology and the Romantic Tradition*, Cambridge MA: Harvard University Press.

Butler, M. (ed) (1993) *Mary Shelley: Frankenstein or The Modern Prometheus. The 1818 Text*, Oxford: Oxford University Press.

Buxton, R. (1994) *Imaginary Greece. The Contexts of Mythology*, Cambridge: Cambridge University Press.

Byrne, S. (ed) (1997) *Tony Harrison. Loiner*, Oxford: Oxford University Press.

Camp, J. (2001) *Archaeology of Athens*, New Haven: Yale University Press.

Cantor, P.A. (1984) *Creature and Creator. Myth-making and English Romanticism*, Cambridge: Cambridge University Press.

Coby, P. (1987) *Socrates and the Sophistic Enlightenment*, Lewisburg, PA: Bucknell University Press.

Conacher, D.J. (1980) *Aeschylus' Prometheus Bound: A Literary Commentary*, Toronto: University of Toronto Press.

Curran, S. (1986) 'The Political Prometheus', *Studies in Romanticism* 15: 429–55.

—— (ed) (1993) *The Cambridge Companion to British Romanticism*, Cambridge, Cambridge University Press.

De Ropp, R.S. (1972) *The New Prometheans: Creative and Destructive Forces in Modern Science*, London: Delacorte Press.

Detienne, M. (1986) *The Creation of Mythology*, trans. M. Cook, Chicago: University of Chicago Press.

Detienne, M. and Vernant, J.-P. (1974) *Cunning Intelligence in Greek Culture and Society*, trans. J. Lloyd, Chicago/London: University of Chicago Press.

Deubner, L. (1932) *Attische Feste*, Berlin: Akademie-Verlag.

Dodds, E.R. (1973) *The Ancient Concept of Progress*, Oxford: Oxford University Press.

Donoghue, D. (1974) *Thieves of Fire*, New York: Oxford University Press.

Dunbar, N. (ed) (1995) *Aristophanes: Birds*, Oxford: Clarendon Press.

Edelstein, L. (1967) *The Idea of Progress in Classical Antiquity*, Baltimore, MD: Johns Hopkins Press.

Ferrain, A. (2000) 'Homo faber, homo sapiens or homo politicus? Protagoras and the myth of Prometheus', *The Review of Metaphysics* 54.2: 289–319.

Finley, M.I. (1970) *Early Greece: The Bronze and Archaic Ages*, New York: Norton.

Frazer, J.G. (1930) *Myths of the Origin of Fire*, London: Macmillan.

Furley, W.D. (198 1) *Studies in the Use of Fire in Ancient Greek Religion*, New York: Arno Press.

Gibbs, L. (trans.) (2002) *Aesop's Fables*, Oxford: Oxford University Press.

Geertz, C. (1973) *The Interpretation of Cultures*, New York: Basic Books.

Grene, D. (trans.) (1956) *Aeschylus II*, Chicago/London: University of Chicago Press.

Griffith, M. (1977) *The Authenticity of* Prometheus Bound, Cambridge: Cambridge Press.

—— (1983a) 'Personality in Hesiod', *Classical Antiquity* 2: 37–65.

—— (ed.) (1983b) *Aeschylus. Prometheus Bound*, Cambridge: Cambridge University Press.

—— (2002) 'Slaves of Dionysos: Satyrs, Audience, and the Ends of the *Oresteia*', *Classical Antiquity* 21: 195–258.

Guthrie, W.K.C. (ed.) (1956) *Plato, Protagoras and Meno*, Baltimore: Penguin Books.

—— (1957) *In the Beginning: Some Greek Views on the Origins of Life and the Early State of Man*, Ithaca: Cornell University Press.

Hall, E. (2002) 'Tony Harrison's Prometheus: A View from the Left:, *Arion* 10.1: 129–40.

Hardwick, L. (2000) *Translating Words. Translating Cultures*, London: Duckworth.

Harrison, T. (1996) *The Labourers of Herakles*, in *Plays 3*, London: Faber and Faber.

—— (1998) *Prometheus*, London: Faber and Faber.

Harth, M.L. (ed) (2001) *José Clemente Orozco. Prometheus*, Claremont, CA: Pomona College Museum of Art.

Henderson, J. (ed. and trans.) (1998) *Aristophanes*, Cambridge, MA: Harvard Classical Library.

Herington, C.J. (1963) 'A Study in the Prometheia', *Phoinix* 17: 236–43.

—— (1970) *The Author of the Prometheus Bound*, Austin: University of Texas Press.

Hope, A.D. (1966) *Collected Poems 1930–1965*, New York: Viking Press.

Hughes, T. (2003) *Collected Poems*, ed. P. Keegan, London: Faber.

Hynes, W. and Doty, W. (eds) (1993) *Mythical Trickster Figures: Contours, Contexts, and Criticisms*, Tuscaloosa/London: University of Alabama Press.

Janik, V. (ed) (1998) *Fools and Jesters in Literature, Art, and History*, Westport, CT: Greenwood Press.

Kelleher, J. (1996) *Tony Harrison*, Plymouth: Northcote House.

Kerényi, C. (1956) 'The Trickster in Relation to Greek Mythology', in Radin 1956.

—— (1963) *Prometheus: Archetypal Image of Human Existence*, trans. R. Manheim, Princeton: Princeton University Press.

Kolakowski, L. (1978) *Main Currents of Marxism*, trans. P. S. Falla, Oxford: Clarendon Press.

Kyle, Donald G. (1987) *Athletics in Ancient Athens*, Leiden: E.J. Brill.

Lamberton, R. (1988) *Hesiod*, New Haven: Yale University Press.

Lehman, J. (1937) *Prometheus and the Bolsheviks*, London: Shenval Press.

Lewis, L. (1992) *The Promethean Politics of Milton, Blake, and Shelley*, Columbia, MO: University of Missouri Press.

Lincoln, B. (1999) *Theorizing Myth*, Chicago: University of Chicago Press.

Lissarrague, F. (1990) 'Why Satyrs are Good to Represent', in J.J. Winkler and F.I. Zeitlin, (eds), *Nothing to Do With Dionysos?*, Princeton: Princeton University Press, 228–36.

Lloyd-Jones, H. (2003) 'Zeus, Prometheus, and Greek Ethics', *Harvard Studies in Classical Philology* 101: 49–72.

Lombardo, S. (trans.) (1993) *Hesiod's Works and Days and Theogony*, Indianapolis/Cambridge: Hackett Pub. Co.

McGann, J.J. (ed) (1986) *Lord Byron. The Complete Poetical Works*, Oxford: Clarendon Press.

Martin, R.P. (1992) 'Hesiod's Metanastic Poetics', *Ramus* 21.1: 11–33.

—— (2003) *The Myths of the Ancient Greeks*, New York: New American Library.

Middleton, C. (ed) (1983) *Johann Wolfgang von Goethe. Selected Poems*, Boston: Suhrkamp/Insel Publishers.

Miller, C.L. (1978) 'The Prometheus Story in Plato's *Protagoras*', *Interpretation: A Journal of Political Philosophy* 7.2: 22–32.

Mitzman, A. (2003) *Prometheus Revisited*, Boston/Amherst: University of Massachusetts Press.

Nagy, G. (1990) *Greek Mythology and Poetics*, Ithaca: Cornell University Press.

Panofsky, D. and Panofsky, E. (1956) *Pandora's Box*, New York: Pantheon Books.

Pelton, R. (1980) *The Trickster in West Africa*, Berkeley/Los Angeles/London: University of California Press.

Radin, P. (1956) *The Trickster*, New York: Philosophical Library.

Radt, S. (ed) (1985) *Tragicorum graecorum fragmenta* III, Gottingen: Vandenhoeck & Ruprecht.

Raggio, O. (1958) 'The Myth of Prometheus: Its Survival and Metamorphoses up to the Eighteenth Century', *Journal of Warburg and Courtauld Institutes*, 21: 44–62.

Raizis, M.B. (1983) *From Caucasus to Pittsburgh: The Prometheus Theme in British and American Poetry*, Athens: Gnosis Pub. Co.

Reid, J.D. (ed.) (1993) *The Oxford Guide to Classical Mythology in the Arts, 1300–1990s*, New York: Oxford University Press.

Ricketts, M.L. (1965) 'The North American Indian Trickster', *History of Religions* 5: 327–50.

Robertson, N. (1985) 'The Origin of the Panathenaea', *Rheinisches Museum für Philologie* 128: 231–95.

Robinson, C.E. (1976) *Shelley and Byron: The Snake and Eagle Wreathed in Flight*, Baltimore/London: Johns Hopkins University Press.

Rosenthal, N. (2003) 'Prometheus's Vulture and the Stem-cell Promise', *New England Journal of Medicine* 349.3: 267–74.

Saïd, S. (1985) *Sophiste et tyran ou le problème du Prométhée enchainé*, Paris: Klincksieck.

Séchan, L. (1951) *Le mythe de Prométhée*, Paris: Presses Universitaires de France.

Sharpe, L. (ed.) (2002) *Cambridge Companion to Goethe*, Cambridge: Cambridge University Press.

Shear, T.L. (1993) 'The Persian Destruction of Athens', *Hesperia* 62.4: 383–482.

Small, C. (1972) *Mary Shelley's Frankenstein: Tracing the Myth*, Pittsburgh, PA: University of Pittsburgh Press.

Snodgrass, A. (1980) *Archaic Greece: The Age of Experiment*, London/Berkeley: University of California Press.

Sommerstein, A. (ed) (1987) *Aristophanes. Birds*, Warminster: Aris & Phillips Ltd.

Sterett, J.R.S. (1901) 'The Torch-Race: A Commentary on the *Agamemnon* of Aischylos vv. 324–326', *American Journal of Philology* 22.4: 393–419.

Sussman, L. (1978) 'Workers and Drones: Labor, Idleness, and Gender Definition in Hesiod's Beehive', *Arethusa* 11: 27–41.

Sutton, D. (1980) *The Greek Satyr Play*, Meisenheim am Glan: Hain.

Tandy, D. and Neale, W.C. (1996) *Hesiod's Works and Days: A Translation and Commentary for the Social Sciences*, Berkeley: University of California Press.

Thompson, H.A. (1981) 'Athens faces Adversity', *Hesperia* 50.4: 343–55.

Thomson, G. (1972) *Aeschylus and Athens*, New York: Haskell House Publishers.

Travlos, J. (1971) *A Pictorial Dictionary of Athens*, New York: Praeger.

Trott, Nicola, (1998) 'Milton and the Romantics', in D. Wu (ed.) *A Companion to Romanticism*, London: Blackwell, 520–34.

Trousson, R. (1976) *Le thème de Prométhée dans la littérature européenne*, Geneva: Droz.

Vernant, J-.P. (1980) 'The Myth of Prometheus in Hesiod', in *Myth and Society*, trans. J. Lloyd, Brighton, Sussex: Harvester Press/Atlantic Highlands, NJ: Humanities Press, 183–201.

—— (1986) 'At Man's Table: Hesiod's Foundation Myth of Sacrifice' in M. Detienne and J.-P. Vernant (eds) *The Cuisine of Sacrifice among the Greeks*, trans. P. Wissig, Chicago/London: University of Chicago Press, 21–86.

Wasserman, E.R. (1971) *Shelley: A Critical Reading*, Baltimore/London: Johns Hopkins University Press.

Watkins, C. (1995) *How to Kill a Dragon: Aspects of Indo-European Poetics*, New York: Oxford University Press.

Webster, T.B.L. (1972) *Potter and Patron in Classical Athens*, London: Methuen.

West, M.L. (ed.) (1966) *Hesiod. Theogony*, Oxford: Oxford University Press.

—— (ed.) (1978) *Hesiod. Works and Days*, Oxford: Oxford University Press.

Wu, D. (ed.) (1998) *A Companion to Romanticism*, London: Blackwell.

Zeitlin, F. (1996) 'Signifying Difference: The Case of Hesiod's Pandora', in *Playing the Other*, Princeton: Princeton University Press, 53–86.

Zillman, L.J. (ed) (1968) *Shelley's Prometheus Unbound: The Text and the Drafts*, New Haven: Yale University Press.

INDEX